Have you ever met a Babylonian? Or a Hittite or an Assyrian ... or a Philistine or an Amalekite?
At one time these were great nations; today they are extinct. When the Jews were captives of the Babylonians, the Jews numbered fewer than 100,000 whereas their captors were innumerable and ruled the world. The Babylonians have sunk beneath the sands of time, but the Jews live on—over 4 million in Palestine alone, just as God promised. Is that a "coincidence"? No! It's one of the signs of the end. And there are many more ...

THE
BEGINNING
OF THE
END

Revised and
Expanded Edition

TIM LaHAYE

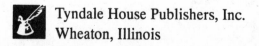

Tyndale House Publishers, Inc.
Wheaton, Illinois

Library of Congress Catalog Card Number 91-65552
ISBN 0-8423-0264-6
© 1972 by Tyndale House Publishers, Inc.
Revised edition © 1991 by Tim LaHaye

99 98 97 96 95 94
9   8   7   6   5   4

CONTENTS

DEDICATION

This book is lovingly dedicated to the memory of the late Dr. David L. Cooper, Th.M., Ph.D., founder of the Biblical Research Society, under whom the author was privileged to study for several years. He provided the germinating thoughts that, after many years, have culminated in this book. His "Golden Rule of Interpretation" has been applied as carefully as possible in an attempt to compare Scripture with present-day fulfillments of prophecy, that hopefully many Christians might be inspired in these last days to be ready when Christ comes.

THE GOLDEN RULE OF INTERPRETATION

When the plain sense of Scripture makes common sense, seek no other sense, but take every word at its primary, literal meaning unless the facts of the immediate context clearly indicate otherwise.

David L. Cooper

INTRODUCTION

As we approach the beginning of the second millennium since Jesus Christ's return to heaven, world events are beginning to move rapidly in fulfillment of the Old and New Testament prophets. Knowledgeable prophecy students are serious in suggesting that we are nearer the beginning of the end of the Church age and the start of those traumatic events foretold by our Lord and his prophets.

Ever since August 2, 1990, the day Saddam Hussein marched 150,000 of his battle-hardened troops into the helpless little country of Kuwait, there has been an intense new interest in Bible prophecy. And well there should be — for the world will never again be the same!

It was not just a matter of "blood for oil," as some peacenik demonstrators would have us believe, because it made this oil-dependent world realize how vulnerable this world is to a ruthless madman obsessed with the idea of world conquest — in the mold of his adopted patron saint, Nebuchadnezzar, of whom Saddam Hussein thought he was the reincarnation.

President Bush's prompt and seemingly unexpected action of sending 450,000 United States troops into Saudi Arabia thwarted Hussein's bold attempt to steal 50 percent of the world's oil and blackmail the world into bankruptcy. Fortunately, this ruthless grab for raw power and dominance by one of the most evil men of this generation ended in failure, as a result of the responsible intervention of the allied forces and by the most awesome display of air power in world history.

If he had succeeded, the price of oil would have shot up to forty or fifty dollars a barrel—making Iraq the richest country in the world. But it would also have destroyed the economies of most Western countries, particularly Germany and Japan, and it would have plunged the poverty-stricken third world countries into hopeless financial destruction and chaos. If unchecked, Saddam would eventually have threatened even the United States and the Soviet Union, not to mention the tiny state of Israel, which would have been totally obliterated in the worst holocaust in the history of mankind.

Saddam Hussein was not the Antichrist, called "the King of Fierce Countenance," but he was almost his equal in craven barbarity. In fact, he is a good study to establish what kind of person the Antichrist will be when he does come—which, if present world events would indicate, can't be too far into the future. Both are egomaniacs and totally amoral with no regard for human life—even the lives of their own countrymen. And like Saddam Hussein, the Antichrist will not be a king nor run for public office, but by sheer ruthlessness he will gain control of one country after another.

THE SIGNIFICANCE OF AUGUST 2, 1990

It is almost impossible to exaggerate the significance of "the Butcher of Baghdad's" march into oil-rich but helpless Kuwait. Not only from a geopolitical point of view, even though it has already changed the world irreversibly, but also prophetically speaking, it has focused the eyes of the world

on the Middle East — the very place where the Hebrew prophets predicted the major end-time events would occur.

Iraq is one of the most ancient countries of the world,
known as Babylon in the Old Testament. It occupies a prominent place in Scripture as "the cradle of civilization," the location of the Garden of Eden, and the ancient city of Babylon —
the most significant city in the world for millennia. Babylon
was the source of most of the world's great evils from false
religions to dictatorial governments. It is one ancient city that
has a future, for Revelation 17 and 18 indicate it will be resurrected from the trash heap of history. Saddam Hussein spent
over $80 million rebuilding the old ruins of Babylon as the
tourist attraction of the world. But that is only the beginning
of the end for the city of Babylon, for it will soon be rebuilt
and become the commercial, banking, and governmental capital of the world. How do we know? Because Revelation 17
and 18 portray its ultimate destruction by God just prior to the
coming of our Lord. Obviously to be destroyed, it must first
be rebuilt.

Saddam Hussein's grab for power and riches points out the
importance of that oil-rich area of the world and gives us a
hint of how easily such a rebuilding of Babylon could be
accomplished. All it would take is the establishment of a
United Nations' "peacekeeping force" in both Iraq and
Kuwait after the removal of the bully of Baghdad. President
Bush and other world leaders have set the stage for just such
an action by calling their allied action "the New World
Order." Once ensconced in power, the U.N. could "annex"
Saudi Arabia's oil, plus that of the emirates, and they would
have the one thing the U.N. has never possessed — a financial
base to accomplish "worldwide good." A ten dollar per barrel
increase in oil would bring tens of billions into the U.N.
coffers — and the potential to raise it to fifty dollars per barrel

is also there. Rebuilding Babylon as the ultimate capital of
"the New World Order" would be feasible. With the civil
unrest in New York City, every day that passes makes such a
move more appealing. In a breathtakingly brief period of time,
such an undertaking could make Babylon the most powerful
and richest country in the world. Modern architecture and
technology could easily make her the capital city of the world,
called "Babylon the Great" that "sits like a queen" described
by the prophet John (Revelation 17 and 18) that will sit on the
treasures and commerce of the world and be the seat of the
Antichrist's kingdom.

THE PROPHETIC "SIGNS" OF THE END

Everyone is interested in the future! Today more than ever,
faced as we are with the threat of nuclear holocaust, international terrorism, worldwide famine, population saturation,
interplanetary space travel, mysterious flying objects, and
international hostilities between nations and races, everyone is
asking serious questions about the future. The bulk of these
revolve around the central question, "How much longer does
man have on this planet?"

No longer does one have to be a "prophet of gloom" or a
doomsayer to foresee that world conditions demand a climax.
Today even the pragmatists are anticipating the end; in fact,
they are trying to prepare for it with warning systems, survival
kits, and training programs. Some have even suggested the
preservation of the finest specimens of our human species to
start the entire human process over again.

Our Lord and his disciples challenged Christians to "discern the times" or read current events in the light of prophecy
so his coming and the end of the age would not overtake
them "as a thief" or unawares. Our generation has seen the

fulfillment of more signs than any generation in the history of the church. Consequently, we have more scriptural evidence for believing Christ could come in our lifetime than any generation of Christians since our Lord ascended into heaven. Some of these signs, like Israel being drawn back into the Holy Land just forty-three years ago after almost nineteen hundred years of wandering around the world without a homeland, are extremely significant. It was only seventy years ago that Russia began to be a dominant world power as the Bible predicted twenty-five hundred years ago. Other signs are even more current. And while we are forbidden to set dates — for as our Lord said, "No man knows the day or the hour" — we can know the "season." Many Bible scholars believe we are living in "the season."

The big problem is, no one knows when the end will be or how it will come. Suggestions vary from today to one hundred years from now. But nothing is definite. It is rather interesting that the closer we get to the year 2000, the more anxious people become about the future and the more widespread grows the universal feeling of "doom." Whether mystics from India or prophetesses from Washington, human soothsayers seem to focus their prophecies near the end of this century. Doubtless the same form of hysteria ushered in the year A.D. 1000, but the twilight of this second millennium since Christ introduces problems never dreamed of during the 970s and 980s.

Although I am not a prophet, nor the son of a prophet, I am not the least reluctant to predict that the next thirty years will find man's hysteria to know the future reaching an all-time fever pitch. Don't be astonished if "false prophets" and "false Christs" spring up all over the world. And don't be astonished if millions of trusting souls follow them to foolishness. For the Bible predicts that such charlatans will come

and "deceive *many.*" We can excuse the feeling of anxiety in
non-Christians, for they don't know any better, but there is
absolutely no excuse for Christians to be "taken unawares"
regarding the end of this age. I don't mean that all Christians
will understand the many intricate details of Bible prophecy,
but there are certain clear events forecast in the Scriptures that
any child of God can comprehend. If he keeps these in focus,
he will not be swept along in any future wave of mass hysteria.

I trust that this book will present both the elementary prophecies regarding the end of this age and some of the more complex predictions in such a practical manner that all may
understand. As this book will attempt to show, we could well
be the generation that sees the culmination of the ages and the
ushering in of the Kingdom of Christ. Certainly we have more
historical evidence for such a possibility than any generation
of Christians in almost two thousand years. In fact, I believe
the Bible teaches that we are already living in the beginning
of the end. My reasons for saying so are found in the following chapters . . . see if you agree.

ONE
THE ABSOLUTE CERTAINTY OF CHRIST'S RETURN

The most significant single truth in all biblical prophecy is the certainty of the Second Coming of Jesus Christ. That event is the prophetic key that unlocks all other future events. It fulfills both the Old and New Testament, including many of Christ's own prophecies; it completes his work of salvation begun during his first coming; and it starts God's prophetic clock of the future. Actually, his Second Coming begins a chain of more than fifteen events, and it is possible to predict the sequence leading to the end of this world after Christ comes. That specific time is unknown to us, for Jesus said of it, "But of that day and hour knoweth no man, no, not the angels of heaven, but my Father only." Although we may speculate on the time when our Lord will reappear, absolutely no question exists that he will come again!

That fact is the primary reason no Christian should be anxious about the end of this age or the chaotic times in which we live. I am frequently asked at prophecy conferences, "Will the world be destroyed by an atomic holocaust?" Naturally, this question is motivated by fear for one's personal safety. Let me put you at ease immediately. Although this world will be destroyed some day (and perhaps by a gigantic nuclear explosion—see 2 Peter 3:10-16), it will not be accomplished by man, but by God himself. Furthermore, the earth will not be destroyed until after Jesus Christ comes back to this earth. In fact, the complete destruction of this world won't take place for more than a thousand years after he comes (see Revelation 19:11–20:10).

Jesus Christ has established himself as the most important person who ever lived, for certainly no other man has influenced humanity to such an extent. He is gone, but he is not through with this planet or the people on it. Before he left the world, he gave an unconditional promise to his followers: "I will come again!" (John 14:3). There is no way that promise can be set aside or explained away. Even if some ingenious scholar could make that promise mean something else, it is repeated so many ways that the promise cannot be nullified.

If the value of a teaching were to be judged by the frequency of its mention, then the Second Coming of Christ would easily rank as one of the most important doctrines in the Bible. Only the subject of salvation is referred to more. Since the 216 chapters of the New Testament contain 318 references to his Second Coming, one verse out of every thirty gives this reassurance.

To help the reader appreciate the New Testament's emphasis on the coming of Christ, I would like to take you on a quick tour of the book-by-book message.

Matthew. Two entire chapters, 24 and 25, are devoted to this subject. Often called "the Olivet Discourse," it was delivered just prior to our Lord's death. This passage contains the most important and complete chronology of future events found in Scripture, with the exception of the book of

Revelation. Consider this description of the Second Coming by Christ himself:

> *Immediately after the tribulation of those days shall the sun be darkened, and the moon shall not give her light, and the stars shall fall from heaven, and the powers of the heavens shall be shaken. And then shall appear the sign of the Son of man in heaven; and then shall all the tribes of the earth mourn, and they shall see the Son of man coming in the clouds of heaven with power and great glory. And he shall send his angels with a great sound of a trumpet, and they shall gather together his elect from the four winds, from one end of heaven to the other. (24:29-31)*

Mark. Although the author compresses the life of Christ into sixteen chapters, he devotes one of them, chapter 13, to the Olivet prophecies of the end times, culminating in the Second Coming of Christ.

Luke. The great first-century historian, Dr. Luke, included the Second Coming prophecies in two chapters, 17 and 21. Consider these words: "And then shall they see the Son of man coming in a cloud, with power and great glory" (21:27).

John. The "Beloved Disciple," who outlived all the other apostles, wrote his life of Christ about fifty years after Christ ascended into heaven. Although he does not repeat the Olivet prophecy covered by the other three Gospel writers, he quotes one of the clearest promises to come from the Savior's lips on this subject:

> *Let not your heart be troubled; ye believe in God, believe also in me. In my Father's house are many mansions; if it were not so, I would have told you. I go to*

*prepare a place for you. And if I go and prepare a place
for you, I will come again, and receive you unto myself,
that where I am, there ye may be also. (14:1-3)*

Acts. Dr. Luke's excellent record of the work of the Holy
Spirit through the lives of the apostles contains several promises of Christ's Second Coming. The first act of the ascended
Christ after arriving in heaven was to dispatch two angelic
messengers who announced to his disciples: "Ye men of Gali-
lee, why stand ye gazing up into heaven? This same Jesus,
which is taken up from you into heaven, shall so come in like
manner as ye have seen him go into heaven" (1:11).

The first sermon Peter preached after the day of Pentecost
records this promise given to the Jews of Jerusalem, many of
whom had doubtless participated in calling for the death of
Christ: "Repent ye therefore, and be converted, that your sins
may be blotted out, when the times of refreshing shall come
from the presence of the Lord; and he shall send Jesus Christ,
which before was preached unto you" (3:19,20).

Thirteen Epistles of Paul. The writings of the apostle
Paul probably had a greater impact on the early church than
those of any other single human being. These epistles, read
and reread in the churches, were accepted on the same plane
as the Old Testament Scriptures (2 Peter 3:15-16). Paul
imparted deep doctrinal teaching, practical exhortation, cor-
rection, and instruction on many aspects of the Christian
life. Thirteen times he mentioned baptism, and only twice
did he touch on communion, yet he mentioned the Second
Coming of our Lord fifty times. As we will distinguish later,
some of the passages refer to Jesus' appearance only to
believers, and other passages to his later appearance before
all mankind.

First Thessalonians is considered the first letter Paul wrote.

In it he referred these young believers to the Second Coming of Christ in every chapter! (See 1:10; 2:19; 3:13; 4:13-18; 5:2, 23.) He repeated that emphasis in even greater detail in 2 Thessalonians (see 1:7-10; 2:1-12; 3:5). These epistles demonstrate how early and insistently Paul taught new converts the doctrine of Christ's return, for he was in their city only three weeks before angry Jews drove him out.

The apostle's love of the Second Coming is seen in his rather stern words at the conclusion of 1 Corinthians: "If any man love not the Lord Jesus Christ, let him be Anathema, Maranatha" (16:22).

The word *maranatha* means "the Lord is coming." That expression gained popularity in the first century and became a common mode of greeting and parting. Christians often included it in letters, and in some cases even soldiers used it as a slogan when they went off to war.

The first century was the most fervent and evangelistic generation the nineteen centuries of church history have yet produced. Christianity established such a foothold in the pagan world that by the third century it was acknowledged as the state religion of Rome. By contrast, with all our sophisticated means of communication, the twentieth-century church's program of evangelization lags behind the birth rate. If we possessed the same confident expectation as the "Maranatha" Christians, we could doubtless reach our generation for Christ. But strangely enough, the closer we get to the actual coming of Christ, the less confident the church seems to be about his coming.

As a teacher of prophecy for more than twenty years, I can recall many "sleeping Christians" who were suddenly "turned on" when the truth of Christ's imminent coming gripped them. Churchianity doesn't motivate anyone, but the "Maranatha" concept does. It makes carnal, cold, and indifferent believers "fervent in spirit." I suggest that each night before going to bed you read some of the Bible passages on the Lord's coming and then go to sleep thinking about them. Before a month is past you will gain a new spark in your life and new fervency in your heart. Maranatha!

The story is told of an old Scottish minister who passed the home of a parishioner on his way to church on Sunday morning. Obviously, the man chopping wood by the side of the house was not going to church. Their eyes met and the pastor felt he should say something, so he called out, "The Lord is coming," and went on to church. About five minutes after he started his message the farmer entered. After the service he admitted, "Pastor, the more I thought about the Lord coming, the more I realized I didn't want him to find me cutting wood during church time." No wonder John said, "Every man that hath this hope in him purifieth himself, even as he is pure" (1 John 3:3).

All but two of Paul's epistles contain one or more references to the Second Coming. It is obliquely cited in Romans 11:26, clearly presented in 1 Corinthians 15 where he expounds upon the resurrection, and mentioned in 2 Corinthians 1:14 and 5:10. Galatians, which offers a deep discussion of the finished work of Christ on the cross, does not contain a clear reference to the Second Coming, though an allusion to the event appears in 1:4. Ephesians presents the Christian "in the heavenlies," and "the day of redemption" (1:14; 4:30) can only mean the day of deliverance through Christ's return. Philippians contains several references to the Lord's coming, the best of which is Philippians 3:20-21:

> For our citizenship is in heaven, from whence also we look for the Savior, the Lord Jesus Christ, who shall change our vile body, that it may be fashioned like unto his glorious body, according to the working whereby he is able even to subdue all things unto himself.

A thrilling promise appears in Colossians: "When Christ, who is our life, shall appear, then shall ye also appear with him in glory" (3:4).

Like 1 and 2 Thessalonians, the epistles to Timothy provide many references to the coming of Christ. In fact, they contain two of the signs, being fulfilled today, that show that we are already in the "last days." We shall study those later. In addition, 2 Timothy 1:10 and 4:1, 8 refer to "his appearing."

The book of Titus contains the advice of a veteran servant of God to a young preacher on how to conduct the work of the Lord in the Church. Paul challenges him to teach the people to deny themselves "ungodliness, and worldly lusts . . . and live soberly, righteously, and godly, in this present world" (2:12).

When all the books of Paul are considered, we find that only two of thirteen omit the Second Coming doctrine, and one of these is Philemon, a personal letter of only one chapter. There is no question the apostle Paul was absolutely certain that his Lord and Savior was coming back to this earth again.

Hebrews. This is a magnificent presentation of Christ as the fulfillment of the Old Testament types and symbols. One of the promises of our Lord's return found in this book states: "So Christ was once offered to bear the sins of many; and unto them that look for him shall he appear the second time without sin unto salvation" (9:28).

James. This little book, which challenges Christians to show their faith by their works, culminates with a strong appeal relative to the coming of Christ: "Be ye also patient, stablish your hearts; for the coming of the Lord draweth nigh" (5:8).

Peter. Writing to the Church while it was undergoing trials of persecution, the apostle Peter challenged the elders to be faithful leaders on the basis of the Lord's coming: "And when the chief Shepherd shall appear, ye shall receive a crown of glory that fadeth not away" (1 Peter 5:4).

Peter's second epistle contains a lengthy prophecy concerning the rise of scoffers in the days just preceding Christ's coming. He promises that in spite of their ridicule, "the day of the Lord will come as a thief in the night" (2 Peter 3:10).

First John. The beautiful epistle that brings assurance and confidence to the believer also challenges him to holy living on the basis of Christ's coming. One example: "And now, little children, abide in him, that, when he shall appear, we may have confidence and not be ashamed before him at his coming" (2:28).

Jude. This one-chapter book contains a quotation from the patriarch Enoch, who walked in intimate fellowship with God during the chaotic days preceding the flood and suddenly went directly to be with God. Genesis 5:24 says, "And Enoch walked with God, and he was not; for God took him." Some prophecy teachers suggest that his experience is symbolic of what will happen to Christians just before the chaotic days of the tribulation period, when the Lord will suddenly take Christians off this earth to be with himself. This is called the Rapture of the Church (see 1 Thessalonians 4:13-18 and 1 Corinthians 15:51-52). Before Enoch's "rapture" or sudden departure, he gave this inspired prophecy: "And Enoch also, the seventh from Adam, prophesied of these, saying, Behold, the Lord cometh with ten thousands of his saints, to execute judgment upon all, and to convict all that are ungodly among them of all their ungodly deeds which they have ungodly committed, and of all their hard speeches which ungodly sinners have spoken against him" (Jude 14-15).

Revelation. The Bible ends with an entire book on prophecy. It directs us to a study of things forecast from the first century after Christ's ascension until the end of the world. Some people erroneously call it the Revelation of Saint John, but he is just the penman. Its prophecies are far too complex for a mere Galilean fisherman. It is really the revelation of Jesus Christ, for it shows his future unveiling as the glorious King of creation.

The following summary notes the revelational periods of the book.

Chapter 1 — Christ's present heavenly glory.

Chapters 2-3 — Christ's relationships with the Church's seven ages from A.D. 30 to the Rapture.

Chapters 4-18 — Christ's role in the seven-year tribulation period.

Chapters 19-20 — Christ's majestic appearance on earth and the establishment of his thousand-year kingdom of peace. This is the event foretold by all the prophets in the Old Testament.

Chapters 21-22 — Christ's destruction of the earth and the establishment of his everlasting kingdom. An intense study of these two chapters brings great hope and inspiration.

There are so many references to Christ's coming in this book that space does not permit a tabulation. And the last chapter gives Christ's specific endorsement of the book. It is as though he put his personal signature beneath its contents by saying: "I, Jesus, have sent mine angel to testify unto you these things in the churches. I am the root and the offspring of David, and the bright and morning star" (22:16).

The last challenge to believers in all ages is, "He which testifieth these things saith, Surely, I come quickly. Amen. Even so, come, Lord Jesus" (22:20). The word *quickly* does not refer to John's day; rather, Jesus will come "suddenly." Every generation of Christians should expect the Lord to come "suddenly."

Although we have included many of the outstanding references to the Lord's Second Coming as found from Matthew to Revelation, this is by no means comprehensive. Our further study will give you an appreciation for the tremendous amount of material God has provided in his Word to establish the absolute certainty of his Son's coming back to this earth.

In summary, twenty-three of the twenty-seven books of the New Testament refer to our Lord's coming to earth again. Of the four books that omit it, the reader should understand that three are single-chapter letters originally written to a particular person about a subject not involved with the Second Coming. Of those books introduced for general use, only one, Galatians, does not specifically refer to it, although, as noted, an implication is present.

The sheer weight of evidence leads to the conclusion that if one believes the Bible, he must believe in the Second Coming of Christ. Not only was it a universal conviction and motivating factor of the early Church, but all nine authors of the New Testament Scriptures mentioned it. Since they universally accepted so literally our Lord's promise, "I will come again," can we do less?

CHRIST'S COMING IS A DOCTRINAL NECESSITY

The New Testament teaches the return of Christ both directly and indirectly. Several great doctrines are absolutely dependent on the coming again of Christ. For example, the doctrine concerning the resurrection of the human body cannot be fulfilled until Christ comes (1 Corinthians 15:23). The victory of Christ over Satan as promised many times, beginning with Genesis 3:15, will not be completed until he comes again. Even the recognition of loved ones in eternity and the physical proof of our being born into the family of God is not evidenced until his coming.

Beloved, now are we the children of God, and it doth not yet appear what we shall be, but we know that, when he

shall appear, we shall be like him; for we shall see him
as he is. And every man that hath this hope in him
purifieth himself even as he is pure. (1 John 3:2-3)

The most important doctrine in all the Scriptures, the one upon which all others depend, is the deity of Jesus Christ. He promised so many times to return that there is simply no way to vindicate his divine nature if he does not come again. God cannot lie or deceive. If Jesus does not come again, he will be guilty of fraud, to say the least. But since that possibility is so incompatible with his earthly life, his promises, and his divine nature, it is beyond possibility. The fact remains that he said, "I will come again!"

A man once asked me, "Don't you have anything better than Christ's own words to prove he is coming again?" I replied, "What could possibly be better than the word of the one who, by the power of his word, created all things?" (Compare Genesis 1 with John 1:3 and Colossians 1:14-20.) Besides, there is nothing so absolute as his Word. Jesus said, "Heaven and earth shall pass away, but my words shall not pass away" (Matthew 24:35).

In the final analysis, it all comes down to what you believe about Jesus Christ, who demanded from Peter's lips the most important response in life: "Whom say ye that I am?" If you believe he is the Son of God, then you have no difficulty accepting his coming. If you don't know him yet as the eternal Son of God, I suggest you concentrate on *him,* not his Second Coming. There is ample reason for believing in his deity on the basis of his resurrection alone. Scripture, history, and human logic cry out to men to accept Jesus Christ as the Son of God, who died for our sins, was buried, and rose again the third day according to the Scriptures (1 Corinthians 15:3-4).

After I spoke on the resurrection of Jesus Christ, I was

confronted with an amazing proposition by a brilliant young physicist with a master's degree from Stanford University. "I am an atheist," he confessed, "but not a scientific atheist." He went on to explain: "I have been taught to thoroughly investigate all sides of a matter before I accept it. So far I have never done that with Christianity. This year I am work-ing as an engineer at General Dynamics Corporation to earn enough money so I can begin working on my Ph.D. program at Brandeis University. Since I am not engaged in academic pursuits this year, I have decided to thoroughly investigate Christianity to see if there is anything credible in it." He added, "I plan to be a college professor and have found that my atheism offers no real philosophy of life to impart to the students. Although I cannot accept the Christians' beliefs, I have observed that the Christian way of life provides a mean-ingful philosophy to pass on to others."

Evidently he had attended the church several times, for he handed me a ten-page analysis of his atheistic doubts and invited me to tutor him in his study of Christianity. As we met regularly that year, I soon found him so methodical that we didn't have time for research on the credibility of the Bible, fulfilled prophecy, or even the full concept of the deity of Christ. After praying about it, I suggested, "Let's concentrate on the bodily resurrection of Jesus Christ." That concept is so basic that its logical proof offers an easy transition to all other Bible doctrines. The young man began to study diligently. Frankly, I was amazed to discover so many books written about the resurrection. He very carefully made two lists, one marked "reasons for accepting the resurrection of Christ," the other, "reasons against Christ's resurrection."

To my dismay, September came and he had not completed his research. When he left for Brandeis University, I thought we had lost him. But to my amazement he came into my office during the Christmas holidays and informed me that he had become a Christian. He then related this story: During the two-day vacation at Thanksgiving he culminated his research and discovered that he had amassed five reasons for accepting the resurrection of Christ for every one against it. "I was forced by the sheer weight of evidence to accept the bodily resurrection of Christ as a historical fact." Then he added, "But that didn't make me a Christian. Suddenly it dawned on me that I had to ask this Christ, in whom I now believed, to come into my life and save me from my sins."

I don't know how many students at the predominantly Jewish Brandeis University have ever knelt by their beds to receive Christ as their Lord and Savior, but my friend is one. Needless to say, it didn't take him long to accept the teaching that one day Jesus Christ will come again.

While reading this book, if you have any doubt as to whether or not you have received Christ as your Lord and Savior, I suggest that you drop to your knees before you read further and ask Christ to come into your heart. The Bible promises, "For whosoever shall call upon the name of the Lord shall be saved" (Romans 10:13).

TWO
RAPTURE OF THE CHURCH

The Second Coming of Jesus Christ is mentioned 318 times in the New Testament alone, but a careful examination of the passages reveals what appears at first to be conflicting concepts. For example, one passage tells us that Christ will come "in the air" (1 Thessalonians 4:17), whereas another tells us he is coming "to the earth." One passage tells us that his coming is to be secret, "as a thief"; another tells us "every eye shall see him." One passage teaches that his coming will be a time of joy and blessing; another tells us the people of the earth shall "mourn."

The only way to correlate these teachings regarding Christ's coming is to understand that his coming is in two stages. The first stage is the Rapture, or taking away, of the Church; the second is the Glorious Appearing to the whole earth. Christ will come secretly in the Rapture and then publicly in the Glorious Appearing. He will come to the sky in the Rapture; he will come to the earth at the Glorious Appearing. The Lord's coming will be a time of great joy when he raptures the Church, but his coming to the earth will be a time of great sorrow, for then he will destroy the wicked nations.

RAPTURE

1 Thess. 4:16-17

CHURCH AGE

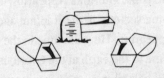

THE SECOND COMING

JUDGMENT SEAT

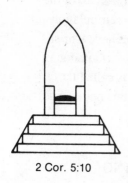

2 Cor. 5:10

GLORIOUS APPEARING

Matt. 24:27-31

GREAT WHITE THRONE JUDGMENT

Rev. 20:11-15

7 YR. TRIBULATION	1000 YR. MILLENNIUM

OF CHRIST

The coming of our blessed Lord is to be a two-stage event, and it is separated by a seven-year interval. This seven years is the fulfillment of the "seventieth week" of Daniel, or the time of "Jacob's trouble." This is called the pretribulation view of our Lord's return. Some Christians believe Christ will rapture the Church after the time of great tribulation or calamities sent by God upon the earth. This is called the posttribulation interpretation, a view which this book finds completely inadequate.

THE TWO STAGES OF JESUS' COMING

Some critics of the pretribulation Rapture assert that no one Bible passage teaches both stages of our Lord's Second Coming. Actually, such passages can be found.

The two stages in one verse. Titus 2:13 speaks of Christians at the Second Coming of Christ "looking for that blessed hope, and the glorious appearing of the great God and our Savior Jesus Christ." The blessed hope is a reference to the Rapture of the Church—the cause for great rejoicing by the Church. The Glorious Appearing, however, refers to the public coming of Christ in his majesty and power to rule the earth. They both refer to the Second Coming but to different stages of that coming.

The two stages in one chapter. Chapter 2 of 2 Thessalonians not only shows both stages of our Lord's return, but the intervening events: the revelation of the Antichrist and the Tribulation period. Verse 1 refers to the coming of our Lord Jesus Christ and "our gathering together unto him." This is an evident reference to the Rapture of the Church, because Christians will come back to earth to rule with Christ at his Glorious Appearing, according to Jude 14-15. Verse 2 then refers to "the Day of the Lord," the time of Christ's punishment of wicked humanity, in which "the heavens shall pass away with a great noise, and the elements will melt with fervent heat" (2 Peter 3:10). This is also the "Glorious Appearing" of Christ. Verse 3 makes it clear that the Day of the Lord will not come until the "man of sin be revealed, the son of perdition." This is the Antichrist. Verse 8 then explains that when Christ comes he will destroy the Man of Sin "with the brightness of his coming."

The sequence of events, then, including the two stages of Christ's Second Coming, is: "our gathering together unto him," the Tribulation persecution and spiritual apostasy when the Man of Sin is revealed, and the Day of the Lord or Glorious Appearing of Christ.

The two stages in one book. The succession of events in the book of Revelation strongly indicates that the Church age described in chapters 2 and 3, of which the writer John is a symbol, is followed by the Rapture of the true Church to heaven, just as John was transported into Christ's presence (4:1-2). The Tribulation then takes place on the earth for seven years, as described in chapters 6 through 18, followed by the Glorious Appearing of Christ to earth pictured in chapter 19.

Thus we see the two separate stages of our Lord's return revealed in one verse, one chapter, and one book of the Scriptures.

It is helpful to keep in mind that there are only two kinds of people on the earth: Christians and unbelievers. Christ's coming will affect each group in different ways at different times. In the first stage for Christians, he will take believers to their heavenly home.

The main Bible passage on the Rapture of the Church is 1 Thessalonians 4:13-18. In this passage believers are told: "Then we which are alive and remain shall be caught up together with them in the clouds." The words "caught up" come from the Greek word *rapture,* which literally means to seize as a robber seizes a prize. The Latin word is *rapto,* meaning to seize forcefully. One day Christ is coming to claim his jewels (that is, his redeemed ones) from the world to take them into heaven with him. This, of course, does not refer to certain denominations or religious groups but to all the individuals who have repented of their sin and have, in faith, invited the Lord Jesus Christ into their life.

Both the living and the dead believers will receive new bodies at the Rapture, as described in 1 Corinthians 15:51-58:

> *Behold, I show you a mystery; We shall not all sleep, but we shall all be changed, in a moment, in the twinkling of an eye, at the last trump: for the trumpet shall sound, and the dead shall be raised incorruptible, and we shall be changed. For this corruptible must put on incorruption, and this mortal must put on immortality. So when this corruptible shall have put on incorruption, and this mortal shall have put on immortality, then shall be brought to pass the saying that is written, Death is swallowed up in victory. O death, where is thy sting? O grave, where is thy victory? The sting of death is sin; and the strength of sin is the law. But thanks be to God, which giveth us the victory through our Lord Jesus Christ. Therefore, my beloved brethren, be ye steadfast, unmovable, always abounding in the work of the Lord, forasmuch as ye know that your labor is not in vain in the Lord.*

"In a moment, in the twinkling of an eye" means our bodies will be transformed as fast as a blinking of the eye. The trumpet shall sound and the dead shall be raised incorruptible, and the living be changed. Notice verse 53, for this corruptible (our temporary bodies) must put on incorruption (or glorified bodies) and this mortal (our flesh) must put on immortality (or glorified bodies). When this happens, "then shall be brought to pass the

saying that is written, Death is swallowed up in victory." The
Christian's final victory is not to be expected in this life, but in
the life to come. Our future with Christ does not depend on
whether a person is alive or dead at the coming of Christ, but
whether he is "in Christ" before he died or before Christ comes;
that is, whether he has voluntarily invited Jesus Christ to come
into his life to be his Savior and Lord.

The details of this great event are seen more clearly in
1 Thessalonians:

> *But I would not have you to be ignorant, brethren, con-
> cerning them which are asleep, that ye sorrow not, even
> as others which have no hope. For if we believe that
> Jesus died and rose again, even so them also which
> sleep in Jesus will God bring with him. For this we say
> unto you by the word of the Lord, that we which are
> alive and remain unto the coming of the Lord shall not
> precede them which are asleep. For the Lord himself
> shall descend from heaven with a shout, with the voice of
> the archangel, and with the trump of God: and the dead
> in Christ shall rise first: then we which are alive and
> remain shall be caught up together with them in the
> clouds, to meet the Lord in the air: and so shall we ever
> be with the Lord. Wherefore comfort one another with
> these words. (1 Thessalonians 4:13-18)*

PAUL'S PURPOSE IN WRITING

The people of Thessalonica were concerned about their
departed loved ones who had put their faith in Christ, thinking
that perhaps they would miss the Rapture. They sent word to
Paul about their concern, and in answering them the Spirit-led
apostle teaches us also.

The passage is written, Paul says, because "I would not have you to be ignorant," and also "that ye sorrow not even as others which have no hope." The Holy Spirit has not said that believers should not sorrow but that we are not to sorrow as the hopeless. Thanks to God, though we grieve to lose our departed loved ones, it is but a temporary separation until we meet together in the Rapture of the Church.

Verse 14 refers to those that "sleep in Jesus." This is an obvious reference to all saints that have died from Pentecost until the Rapture of the Church. This does not refer to their souls or spirits, for the soul involves the emotions, will, and mind, all of which are eternal and never sleep. Both the rich man and Lazarus described by the Lord Jesus in Luke 16 could think (mind), could feel (emotions), and could desire (will) after they died. The Bible never refers to soul sleep.

Verse 15 clearly points out the fact that Paul is not teaching this as his personal opinion, but: "This we say unto you by the word of the Lord."

THE ORDER OF EVENTS

We find seven distinct steps taking place in the "twinkling of an eye" at the Rapture:

> *For the Lord himself shall descend from heaven with a shout, with the voice of the archangel, and with the trump of God: and the dead in Christ shall rise first: then we which are alive and remain shall be caught up together with them in the clouds, to meet the Lord in the air: and so shall we ever be with the Lord. (1 Thessalonians 4:16-17)*

1. "For the Lord himself shall descend." The Lord is not sending the archangel Michael, but our Savior himself is coming for us.

2. "With a shout." The shout for the believer is going to be from the Lord himself, whose voice has already proven its authority to raise the dead. One day, standing at the tomb of Lazarus, who had been dead four days, Jesus shouted, "Lazarus, come forth," and before the eyes of many witnesses Lazarus "came forth." Just as dead Lazarus responded, so all those that sleep in Jesus will respond when he calls.

3. "The voice of the archangel" will lead the Jews through the Tribulation period or the "time of Jacob's trouble."

4. "The trump of God" will signal imminent judgment upon the earth for its gross wickedness. The Tribulation that follows the Rapture is an unparalleled visitation of plagues.

5. "And the dead in Christ shall rise first" is the same as "the dead shall be made incorruptible." All dead Christians will be given a glorified body, which will unite with their soul and spirit. This is called the resurrection of the believer.

6. "Then we which are alive and remain shall be caught up together with them in the clouds." We who happen to be living at the Rapture will be "made incorruptible." Our soul and spirit never leave the body, but suddenly our body becomes "like unto his glorified body," referring to our Lord's resurrection body, and we will immediately leave this earth. No matter what we are doing we will suddenly be taken out of the world.

The Rapture of the Church will be an event of such startling proportions that the entire world will be conscious of our leaving. Some have suggested that there will be airplane, bus, and train wrecks throughout the world when Christian operators are suddenly taken out of the world. Who can imagine the chaos on the freeways when automobile drivers are snatched out of their cars!

One cannot help but surmise that many strangers will be in churches the first Sunday after the Rapture. A gospel-preaching church will probably have a few unsaved members anxiously gathering to tremble together over their destiny. Liberal churches, where heretics in clerical garb have not preached the Word of God and the need for a new-birth experience, may be filled to capacity with wondering and frantic church members. Many a minister will have to "explain it away" in some fantastic manner or seriously alter his theology.

7. "To meet the Lord in the air." It seems that our Lord permits us to meet one another in the clouds before we gather together unto him. What a blessed reunion we will have renewing fellowship with other saints and with loved ones who have passed away before our Lord's coming! Then we will meet our blessed Lord face to face, fulfilling the Scriptures that we will "see him as he is."

A CAUSE FOR COMFORT

"And so shall we ever be with the Lord." What exhilarating words these are, promising that after the Rapture of the Church we will forever enjoy the presence of our Lord. A little girl was asked by a scoffer of the Second Coming of Christ, "How can you enjoy heaven? Christ is supposed to come down to earth!" The scoffer's question bothered her only a moment before she replied, "It really doesn't matter, because wherever he goes I'll go with him!"

"Wherefore, comfort one another with these words" (1 Thessalonians 4:18). There is much comfort to be found and shared with other Christians through this anticipation. The Christians' future is not just bright — it's dazzling!

PREPARATION FOR THE RAPTURE

The wonderful event described in these verses is only for those who have met the condition of verse 14: "If we believe that Jesus died and rose again" — that is, if you have put your trust in the dying and resurrected Savior. If you have never personally trusted in him, you will not join him at his coming.

The selective nature of the Rapture is illustrated by our Lord in Luke 17:34-36:

> *I tell you, in that night there shall be two men in one bed; the one shall be taken, and the other shall be left. Two women shall be grinding together; the one shall be taken, and the other left. Two men shall be in the field; the one shall be taken, and the other left.*

When I was a boy I took a tour of the Henry Ford factory in Dearborn, Michigan. There we saw an electromagnetic crane move over a large railroad car filled with what seemed to be junk steel. At the flip of a switch everything in that car leaped up to the magnetic crane. Then I saw a strange thing: some pieces of steel fell back into the car. Being curious, I waited until others left on the next stage of the tour and then climbed up to look inside and find out why these pieces fell back in. I found they were not steel at all. Lying on the bottom of the car were some old two-by-fours, a broom handle, and some broken pieces of wood. Only those objects that were made of the right components responded to the magnet; the rest were left behind. That is exactly the way it will be when the Lord comes. Those individuals who do not have the Spirit of God within them through faith in Christ will not respond to him at his coming.

If you have the slightest doubt whether you are ready for the Lord Jesus' coming, I suggest that right now you can bow your head and ask Christ into your heart. If you don't know how to pray I suggest the following: "O God, I am a sinner and need the forgiveness you offer in your Son, Jesus Christ. Please come into my life, save me from my past, and become the Lord of my future. I give myself to you."

He will take you all the way.

THREE
THE FIRST SIGN OF THE END

A few years ago a national science journal carried on its cover the startling picture of a clock set at three minutes to twelve. It represented the concept of how close our atomic era was to the end of history. Although disagreeing with their reasons, Bible students do not disagree with their conclusion, for the Bible seems to indicate that man's time on this earth under human government is very limited.

Our reasons for this conclusion are a number of prophecies throughout the Bible that are being fulfilled now or will be in the very near future. These signs of the times follow each other in close succession. We shall look at each sign individually and then examine their accumulative weight, beginning with the first great sign described in Matthew 24 and proceeding in chronological order.

CHRIST'S OLIVET PROPHECY
The most important single prophecy concerning the coming of Christ and the end of this age very fittingly came from

Christ himself. It is not only the most complete coverage of the subject to be found in one passage, but it provides the chronological framework into which all other prophecies must fit to be intelligible. This prophecy is so important that it was included in three of the four Gospels.

To properly understand this prophecy that marks the beginning of the end of this age, we must keep in mind the setting in which it was given. Christ had already predicted his death, which he knew would take place in a matter of days. As was his custom when in Jerusalem, he went into the temple, which he called "my Father's house of prayer," and afterward:

> *Jesus went out, and departed from the temple; and his*
> *disciples came to him for to show him the buildings of*
> *the temple. And Jesus said unto them, See ye not all*
> *these things? Verily I say unto you, there shall not be left*
> *here one stone upon another, that shall not be thrown*
> *down. (Matthew 24:1-2)*

Evidently the disciples were trying to impress Jesus with the beauty of Herod's temple, probably the greatest building south of Rome. But Jesus used the opportunity to convey a preliminary prediction about the temple itself — that it would be destroyed. Note the specific content of this prophecy. He did not say it was only to be destroyed, but that "there shall not be left here one stone upon another, that shall not be thrown down."

THE FULFILLMENT OF JESUS' PROPHECY

History records that this prophecy was fulfilled forty years later. In A.D. 70, armies of Titus surrounded Jerusalem, and after a 143-day siege they destroyed the city, including the temple. We are told that Titus gave the order to preserve all religious buildings in the city, but the soldiers' greed inspired their disobedience to his order. The temple, of course, was the richest treasure in Jerusalem. In fact, an unconfirmed story says the heat from the burning city melted the gold overlay of the temple, much of which seeped into the unmortared joints of the building's massive stones. Since Roman soldiers were paid primarily by what they could plunder, they wanted that gold. To get it, they had to take the temple apart stone by stone.

The fulfillment of the prophecy does not depend on this interesting tradition. Historical fact reveals that the building was destroyed until there was "not one stone upon another." Twice I have been in Jerusalem on the site of the temple of Jesus' day. Not one of the huge stones that made up the temple is on that site, because the Dome of the Rock, the second most holy edifice of the Muslim world, is located there. You can be sure that the Arabs would not allow a trace of the Jewish temple to remain there. The whole world should be familiar with this fulfillment, because the conclusion of the six-day Israel-Arab war produced pictures of Jews rejoicing and weeping at the Wailing Wall, a sad reminder of the once glorious temple. That wall is made up of stones from the temple of Jesus' day, and not one square inch of it rests on the site of the old temple.

THE DISCIPLES' QUESTIONS

After predicting the destruction of the temple, the Lord led his disciples across the valley to one of his favorite places, the Mount of Olives. "And as he sat upon the Mount of Olives, the disciples came unto him privately, saying, Tell us, when shall these things be? And what shall be the sign of thy coming, and of the end of the world?" (Matthew 24:3).

Notice that the disciples asked a three-part question:
1. When shall these things be?
2. What shall be the sign of thy coming?
3. What is the sign of the end of the world?

The disciples were probably familiar with the prophecy of Zechariah 14:1-3, which predicts the destruction of Jerusalem just before the Day of the Lord. Therefore they naturally linked the two events together. Knowing they were concerned about the time of his return and the end of the age, Jesus answered questions two and three first, then answered question one in verses 32-36. In so doing he left us a four-part description of *the sign* of his return to earth and the end or consummation of the age.

JESUS' WARNING

Before giving the sign, our Lord warned his disciples to "take heed that no man deceive you." He predicted two false signs.

"For many shall come in my name, saying, I am Christ; and shall deceive many" (vv. 4-5). History reveals hundreds of false messiahs who, we must confess, have never lacked a following. Some have appeared and blasphemously used the name of Jesus Christ. Others have established cults or religious sects that have left the deceived followers worse off than before.

No Christian who knows the Bible should ever be deceived by such false claims. For when Christ comes we will need no introduction to him, for we will "be like him; for we shall see him as he is" (1 John 3:2). As long as we are in these mortal bodies, Christ has not come. If the messiah we meet has not resurrected the dead and "changed our vile bodies" into "incorruptible bodies," then he isn't our Messiah (1 Corinthians 15:51-53).

The second false sign is wars and rumors of wars. "And ye shall hear of wars and rumors of wars; see that ye be not troubled; for all these things must come to pass, but the end is not yet" (Matthew 24:6). One of my majors in college was history, a subject that has always fascinated me. It didn't take me long to see that a study of human history was basically a study of war. Ever since men rejected Jesus Christ by saying, "We will not have this man reign over us; we have no king but Caesar," they have had Caesars who led them into war after war.

As a newspaper boy in 1940 I went to collect from an elderly customer. She was reading the paper I had left earlier that morning. To my surprise she lashed out at me, "If all you can bring me is news about war, war, war, you can stop delivering this paper!" I have thought about that poor soul and others like her many times since 1940 as we have gone through World War II, Korea, Vietnam, and more than 130 other "wars and rumors of wars." I didn't know the comforting word of Christ to give that troubled customer, but I do now. It's as Jesus said: "When ye shall hear of wars and rumors of wars, see that ye be not troubled."

These words have just taken on new meaning for me as I write them, because my oldest son is going through basic training as a two-year volunteer in the U.S. Army. Like any father who dearly loves his boy, my heart skips a beat each time I read about flare-ups in the Middle East and I wonder if his next visit to Israel will involve him in another of history's "wars and rumors of war." It is certainly a comfort to hear the Lord say, "Let not your heart be troubled." Very honestly, I don't know how non-Christian parents carry such burdens without being able to commit their loved ones to God's mercy and care.

Many years ago a fine minister preached a sermon entitled "Wars and Rumors of Wars — Sign of the Lord's Return." He was a good man, but he was dead wrong! Jesus said, "All these things must come to pass, but the end is not yet." Wars and rumors of wars indicate that we have *not* reached the end of the age. It should be kept in mind, nevertheless, that Jesus did include the subject of war while talking about signs. The reason will be seen in the next verse as he singles out of history a very special war that I believe is *the sign*.

THE SIGN

"For nation shall rise against nation, and kingdom against kingdom; and there shall be famines, and pestilences, and earthquakes, in divers places" (Matthew 24:7).

After noting that the ordinary wars of history were not the sign, the Lord selects one special war that would be that sign. It is a certain kind of war for which he uses a Hebrew idiom.[1] This special war was to be started by two nations getting into a conflict joined by the kingdoms of the world. Since he had a worldwide view here he predicted that two nations would enter a conflict and then be joined by the other kingdoms of the world. But that is only one part of the fourfold sign. Consider all four parts of this one sign:

1. A world war started by two nations;
2. famines;
3. pestilences;
4. earthquakes in various places simultaneously.

Since world history records many famines, pestilences, and earthquakes, together with many wars, there must be something special about these. Like the worldwide war, they probably are unprecedented famines, pestilences, and earthquakes, somehow directly associated with the war.

Now we are ready to ask: Has there ever been a war, started by two nations, which grew into a worldwide war by the kingdoms of the world, followed by unprecedented famines, pestilences, and earthquakes in various places (perhaps simultaneously)? I am of the opinion that we can discern such. Though reluctant to be dogmatic on the subject, I believe there is one event that fulfills all four parts of this prophecy. That terrible event has been labeled by historians as World War I, which took place between 1914 and 1918.

The spark that ignited World War I flared on June 28, 1914, during a state visit to Serbia by the heir-apparent to the Austrian throne, Archduke Francis Ferdinand. A Serbian zealot assassinated the Austrian prince, and after a month of hostilities between the two countries, Austria declared war on Serbia on July 28. Shortly thereafter the kingdoms of the world chose sides and entered the conflict until twenty-seven nations officially declared war. Before it was over, forty-three of the principal nations of the world had been involved. All of the major world powers and a majority of the smaller nations joined one side or the other. In Europe only the Scandinavian countries and Switzerland remained neutral, but some of their citizens fought as volunteers on one side or the other.

Since many who read this book were not living at the time of World War I, we shall quote some statistics to show the immense proportions of that global conflict. Julius Caesar extended the Roman Empire from the Euphrates in Persia to England's Thames with an army of 400,000. The Napoleonic wars covered all Europe except England, Western Asia, and North Africa, yet he had only 750,000 men. It is reported that one out of every seven men on the earth during 1914–1918 was in uniform, totaling 53 million. Although it is impossible to be certain how many soldiers died in battle during that war, General Tasker Bliss estimates that they approximate 13 million. Marshall Robertson adds that those killed in blockades, revolutions, and sunken or shipwrecked boats comes to the staggering figure of 37 million. The financial cost of this conflict has been placed in excess of $337 billion, which in that day exceeded by one-third the estimated wealth of the United States.[2]

Historians agree that World War I was unique in the annals of warfare. One writer said, "World War I differed in many respects from any previous war. It involved literally the whole population of the warring nations. All able-bodied men were recruited or conscripted for combat or munitions factories. Women and children worked in factories. Whole populations were subject to air raids, gas attacks, and the rationing of food, clothing, and other necessities of life. Hence social effects were greater than in previous wars."[3]

The most unique feature of World War I goes beyond these facts. In other great wars one nation was usually the principal aggressor against smaller nations. History records a parade of dictators or kings who inspired their nations to conquest and plunder. Nebuchadnezzar led the Babylonians to victory over many surrounding nations. Alexander the Great led the Greeks, and Julius Caesar led the Romans to widespread empire. Many others have tried: Attila the Hun, Genghis Khan, Napoleon Bonaparte, Adolf Hitler, and more recently Saddam Hussein.

World War I was different. The western powers were divided along nationalistic lines with no great prizes at stake. What started as a conflict between two little countries turned into a world war as the kingdoms of the world joined the fray on one side or the other. Thus World War I fulfilled the prophetic idiom of a worldwide conflict started by two nations.

The events of World War I fulfill only the first part of this four-part sign. To qualify as *the sign* of the end of the age, it must also be followed by unprecedented famines, pestilences, and earthquakes. The almanac and encyclopedias reveal that the aftermath of World War I did indeed produce such unprecedented catastrophes. Famine always follows the ravages of war — the greater the war, the greater the famine. World War I was no exception. "It is a known fact, that as a result of the war and the revolutions which followed, more than 27 million people starved to death."[4] Reports from China, Russia, India, and Europe indicate unusual famine conditions that exceeded any in world history. It should be kept in mind that the socialistic concepts of communism, together with the Communists' penchant for brutality and butchery, have stifled human initiative to such an extent that famine has become a tragic by-product.

Pestilence or life-destroying diseases and plagues usually follow famines. If man's diet is inadequate, he becomes susceptible to many diseases, and statistics show a phenomenal number of deaths after World War I due to tuberculosis, plagues, cholera, typhus, and cancer, to name a few. History books tell of the influenza epidemic that swept through Europe and jumped the Atlantic, killing more American civilians than died on the battlefields of Europe. Some estimates go as high as 28 million deaths due to influenza. An article in the *New York Times,* written twenty years later, said: "It was an undisputed fact that the influenza epidemic has been the greatest pestilence of all history."[5] That epidemic reached its greatest height in 1918.

The fourth part of the sign relates to "earthquakes in various places," or, as some suggest, multiple earthquakes. Even with incomplete records there is little question that earthquakes have been on the increase in this century. I have read statistics that certain earthquakes, like the one in Baluchistan, West Pakistan, on May 31, 1935, was the "most devastating earthquake in all history," but that record has been exceeded several times since then. Major earthquakes have occurred since World War I in such various places as Kansu Province, China; Tokyo, Japan; Persia; India; Peru; Formosa; and southern California. The only known multiple earthquakes in history have been recorded since World War I. For example, during the Turkish earthquake similar reports came in from Africa, South America, South Carolina, and southern California. During a prolonged quake in Helena, Montana, there were similar reports in New York and Honduras.

Comparisons of earthquakes are difficult because only in recent years has the science of seismology been sufficiently advanced to adequately detect and record earth movement. But it is safe to conclude that the years since World War I have contained more major earthquakes than any similar period in history. And the millions who have died because of them could very well exceed the number of earthquake deaths in all preceding history.

Seismologists indicate a very interesting pattern in this connection. Earthquakes have been increasing in number and intensity. Each decade outperforms the previous decade, and even more earthquakes are predicted. It is almost as though the earth is preparing for the cataclysms of the coming Tribulation period and the devastation of much of the earth prior to the coming kingdom age of Christ.

When added together, these facts of history give us ample reason to conclude that the Austrian declaration of war in July 1914 began to fulfill *the sign* of the end of the age as given by our Lord. Although I am open to additional evidence on the subject, I am convinced that the events of 1914–1918 fulfill the beginning of Jesus' prophecy. World War I was unique among conflicts, not only in size and extent, but in the way it started.

That one of a kind war — which our Lord selected from among all the wars in human history to be "the sign of the end

of the age" — changed the world more graphically than any
event in history — save the birth and death of Christ himself. All
the subsequent signs that we shall study grew out of that special
war, which even the world called World War I. No other war
comes close. It was not intended to usher in the coming of
Christ. But like the first birth pain of a woman in labor, it was
intended to teach us to look for additional signs or "birth pains."

Until history produces a more acceptable fulfillment, it is
reasonable to conclude that 1914 ushered in the beginning of
the end. What is incredibly interesting is the fact that most
of the additional signs I shall present in this book grew out of
that First World War sign.

JUST THE BEGINNING

The sign, as described in advance by our Lord, was not
intended to usher in the end. It was merely the beginning of
the end, as we can see through his statement in verse 8: "All
these" — meaning all four parts of the sign — "are the beginning of sorrows." The word would better have been rendered
"travail," as in other translations (American Standard Version).
The word *travail* was not unknown to the disciples, who were
familiar with the Old Testament prophets who had employed
it in conjunction with the time of Tribulation that was to come
upon Israel at the end of the age. A careful reading of Isaiah
66:7-9, Jeremiah 4:23-31, Hosea 13:12-14, and Micah 4:9–5:3
will show that this word was used by the prophets to compare
a woman's travail, or birth pains prior to the birth of her child,
with Israel's travail at the end of the age.

"The beginning of travail" is an idiom easily understood
when we consider natural childbirth. My wife has given birth
to four children. Since we have lived in different parts of the
country, only two were delivered by the same doctor, but all

three of her gynecologists gave us the same medical advice. "When your birth pains start coming, wait until they become sharp and regular. Time them, and when they come consistently at three-minute intervals for a period of ten minutes, head for the hospital." This pattern is not only basic to childbirth but instructive of the time of the end. Not one of those doctors advised us that after the first birth pain we were to look for the birth of the baby. Instead, the first birth pain was the signal that we were to look for the second. Not until they were intensified in severity and regularity were we to look for the child. So Jesus would have us know that after the first sign or birth pain we should look for other birth pains. Like a woman in travail, we would experience several other signs or birth pains that would increase as history brought us closer to the time of his coming. It is my firm belief that that is exactly what has happened since 1914.

My intention is to show that at least eleven other Bible prophecies of the last days have been fulfilled, all of them subsequent to World War I. I shall also show that those astounding events, which we shall consider as worldwide birth pains, have increased in number and severity as we approach the end of this age. Furthermore, I shall present additional scriptural evidence strongly indicating that the coming of Christ is very near at hand.

To graphically convey the lateness of the hour and the relation of each sign or birth pang to the other, we shall use the advancing hands of a clock. The first sign is set at the 10:30 P.M. point in human history. When the eleven other signs are examined, you will have ample evidence that we are rapidly approaching the midnight or closing hour of human history.

In view of this clear warning, confirmed by many perilous conditions throughout the world today, you should ask yourself if you are prepared for Christ at his coming. Part of the reason he gave this prophecy is that you might "watch and be ready, for in such an hour as ye think not the Son of man cometh." We cannot know the day or the hour of his coming, just as a woman cannot tell exactly when her child will be born. She can judge by the increasing birth pains that it is near, but the exact moment of birth comes suddenly. So it will be with our Lord's coming.

If you have any doubt that you have invited Jesus Christ into your life, let me urge you to call upon him right now. God knows your heart and will respond if in simple faith you ask him into your life. If the following prayer expresses the desire of your heart, please use it sincerely.

"O God, I am a sinner. I need Jesus Christ to come into my life and become my Lord and Savior. I give my life to you in Jesus' name."

The Bible assures us: "For whosoever shall call upon the name of the Lord shall be saved" (Romans 10:13).

1. See 2 Chronicles 15:1-7 and Isaiah 19:1-4 as precedents.
2. The statistics were taken from *Why Wars Must Cease,* by ten authors (New York: Macmillan, 1935).
3. *Grolier Encyclopedia,* Vol. 20, p. 60.
4. Wm. Beirnes, "Exposition of the Olivet Discourse," *The Midnight Cry,* p.18.
5. Milton B. Lindberg, quoted in *Is Ours the Closing Generation of the Age?* (Chicago Hebrew Mission, 1938), p. 15.

FOUR
THE INFALLIBLE SIGN

On May 14, 1948, a historical phenomenon appeared that traces its beginning to World War I. Against all human reasoning, a nation that had been dead for nineteen hundred years suddenly came to life. On that day the world unknowingly took a giant step closer to the end of the age, for Israel became a self-governing nation just as the prophets had foretold.

Bible students were not surprised by this development. In fact, so many Scriptures refer to the nationhood of Israel in the last days that godly writers as far back as the sixteenth and seventeenth centuries were bold enough to make such predictions. Naturally, they were laughed at because the Turkish control of Palestine made such a possibility highly unlikely. But Israel's 1948 war for independence and their victorious Six-Day War in 1967 have suspended the laughter. Now skeptics would have us believe that any similarity between prophecy and the established facts of history is just a "coincidence."

What skeptics classify as a coincidence is in reality an infallible sign of the divine authorship of the Scriptures. Who but

God could have inspired writers to make a prediction twenty-five hundred years ago that defies history and human nature and is fulfilled before our eyes!

ISRAEL — A MIRACLE NATION

That the Jewish nation exists today is nothing short of a miracle! After twenty-five hundred years without self-government and eighteen hundred years without a national home, she has every reason to be extinct. In all the annals of history, no other people deprived of their homeland has been able to maintain its identity and "resurrect" its country.

America is a good example of what happens when Englishmen, Swedes, Poles, Frenchmen, and others live together. Slowly but surely there is a blending of the nationalities and races until a new strain emerges. Many countries, such as Mexico and the South American nations, have such a blending in just three or four hundred years until it is difficult to detect the original ancestry. The Jews provide the one international exception. Although scattered all over the world these last eighteen hundred years, exposed to practically every genetic strain that exists, they are still a people with ethnic, social, and religious similarities that no one can fail to identify. Mark Twain, who noted their unique genetic individuality, penned these words:

> He could be vain of himself and not be ashamed of it. Yes, he could be excused for it. The Egyptian, the Babylonian, and the Persian arose, filled the planet with sound and splendor, then faded to dream-stuff, and passed away; the Greek and the Roman followed, and made a fast noise, and they are gone; other peoples have sprung up and held the torch high for a time; but it burned out,

*and they sit in twilight, or have vanished. The Jew saw
them all, and is now what he always was, exhibiting no
decadence, no infirmities of age, no weakening of his
parts, no slowing of his energies, no dulling of his alert,
aggressive mind. All things are mortal but the Jew; all
other forces pass, but he remains. What is the secret of
his immortality?*[1]

The answer to his question is found in the promises of God to
Israel: "The Lord's portion is his people; Jacob is the lot of his
inheritance." "I am the Lord, I change not; therefore ye sons of
Jacob are not consumed" (Deuteronomy 32:9; Malachi 3:6).

During the reign of Russia's Peter the Great, an aged
preacher of the Word was imprisoned because of his testi-
mony for Christ. One night the czar called the aged saint
before him and asked the question, "Can you give me one
infallible proof to verify the Bible?"

The old man said, "Yes, sire, the Jew."

The existence of Jewish people, scattered in most countries
of the earth but maintaining their distinctive nationality, can
be attributed only to the supernatural power and special purpose of God. This phenomenon should convince doubting
individuals that God keeps his promises.

The significance of Israel's existence is better comprehended when compared to other nations. Have you ever met a
Babylonian? Or a Hittite or an Assyrian or a Philistine or an
Amalekite? At one time these were great nations; today they
are extinct. In fact, when the Jews were captives of the Babylonians they numbered much less than 100,000, whereas
their captors were innumerable and ruled the world. The Babylonians have sunk beneath the sands of time, but the Jews live
on — over 4 million in Palestine alone, just as God promised.
Is that really a "coincidence"?

You can be sure of one thing—the advocates of the coincidence theory would be among the first to deride the Bible if there were no distinct Jews to be regathered to the land, because the Bible makes so many predictions about the future of Israel. I am afraid the shallow attempt to explain this miracle away as "coincidence" is symptomatic of the skeptics' preconceived ideas, stubbornly maintained, whenever they look at evidences for the supernatural origin of the Bible— if indeed they ever do. One professor with whom I spoke is probably typical. When asked if he had ever studied the evidence for the Bible's accuracy, he replied, "I didn't know there was any!" When you examine only one side of any evidence, you cannot help but come to a one-sided conclusion.

In recent years a bizarre explanation of Israel's reestablishment arose: the Jews going back to Israel are not really God's chosen people, but a fraudulent group of Kahzars that emerged in the Middle Ages. This concept, which doesn't stand the test of historical scrutiny, has not found wide acceptance. As a student of human temperament for many years, I have been intrigued by the Jewish temperament. After carefully analyzing the temperament of the first Israelite as he is described in the Bible, I have found Jacob to be a "dead ringer" for the twentieth-century residents of Israel.

When all the facts are considered, it is very logical to conclude that Israel's regathering into the land is in direct fulfillment of the promises of God. So numerous are those promises that we do not have space to consider them all here. (For those who wish to study them further, additional passages are Deuteronomy 4:27-31; Isaiah 11:9-12; 60:20; Jeremiah 24:6; Ezekiel 36:22-24; and Amos 9:14-15.) Suffice it to say that a comparison study of those passages would indicate that we may expect two regatherings. The one we are seeing in our day under the direction of world Zionism—this occurs in unbelief. It is a partial regathering which will, as we shall see, give Jews opportunity to rebuild their temple. But it will not be a permanent regathering, for the coming world dictator will desecrate their temple and drive them out of the Holy Land. The second and final regathering, accomplished by Christ himself, will be universal in that all believing Israelites will be included. And they will never again leave the Land of Promise (Ezekiel 36:24-38; 11:17-20).

The current regathering of Israel in unbelief, a necessary event before the end of the age, is another sign that the end is approaching. We shall therefore consider the passage in the Scriptures that gives the greatest detail concerning this future gathering. By comparing recent history with this prophecy, we will again see evidence for believing that the end is close at hand.

VISION OF DRY BONES

The hand of the Lord was upon me, and carried me out in the Spirit of the Lord, and set me down in the midst of the valley which was full of bones, and caused me to pass by them round about. And, behold, there were very many in the open valley, and, lo, they were very dry. And he said unto me: Son of man, can these bones live? And I answered: O Lord God, thou knowest.

Again he said unto me: Prophesy upon these bones; and say unto them: O ye dry bones, hear the word of the Lord. Thus saith the Lord God unto these bones: Behold, I will cause breath to enter into you, and ye shall live. And I will lay sinews upon you, and will bring up flesh upon you, and cover you with skin, and put breath in you, and ye shall live; and ye shall know that I am the Lord. So I prophesied as I was commanded. And as I prophesied,

> there was a noise and, behold, a shaking and the bones
> came together, bone to his bone. And when I beheld, lo,
> the sinews and the flesh came up upon them, and the skin
> covered them above, but there was no breath in them.
>
> Then said he unto me: Prophesy unto the wind, proph-
> esy, son of man, and say to the wind: Thus saith the Lord
> God: Come from the four winds, O breath, and breathe
> upon these slain, that they may live. So I prophesied as
> he commanded me, and the breath came into them, and
> they lived, and stood up upon their feet, an exceeding
> great army. Then he said unto me: Son of man, these
> bones are the whole house of Israel; behold, they say:
> Our bones are dried, and our hope is lost; we are cut
> off for our parts. (Ezekiel 37:1-11)

Ezekiel, chapter 37, presents a very strange vision to the
prophet. He is seen looking down into a valley full of dry
bones. Upon hearing the word of the Lord, he observes this
valley of bones suddenly start to move. The bones find their
natural place, "bone to his bone," sinews (or muscle) cover
them, "and flesh came up; their skin covered them above."
Last of all God breathed "breath" into them. The identity of
these bones cannot be questioned, for in verse 11 we are told,
"Son of man, these bones are the whole house of Israel."
Inasmuch as these bones are pictured as coming to life to form
a great army, and they are identified as "the whole house of
Israel," the only possible explanation is that the nation of
Israel, which for nineteen hundred years has been as a valley
of dry bones, would some day be revived.

It is most interesting to notice the progression of this
chapter. In verse 3 the Lord asks the prophet, "Can these
bones live?" The prophet's answer is obviously that of a
spiritual man, for he replies, "O Lord God, thou knowest."

For twenty-five hundred years man has scoffed at the prediction that the people of Israel would one day have their nation. In A.D. 70 the armies of Titus destroyed the city of Jerusalem and drove the Jews out of the Holy Land. For nineteen hundred years the only evidence that they would one day be gathered existed in the Word of God. Truly it could be said of God, "Only thou knowest." Today, however, the world knows, because the world that lives by sight can see the literal nation of Israel.

The gradual progression of the nation from scattered skeleton to full body development is startling. As Ezekiel's prophecy indicates: "There was a noise and a shaking and the bones came together, bone to his bone." Following this, "the sinews and the flesh came upon them, and the skin covered them above, but there was *no breath* in them" (v. 8). Obviously, from the sound of an earthshaking event the seemingly dead nation of Israel was to *gradually* formulate a body *after* which the spirit would be breathed into the nation. I submit that history records the birth of the nation of Israel exactly in this manner, beginning in 1917.

The late Bible scholar Dr. David L. Cooper used to tell this story. He was a young man during World War I and clearly remembered the events. By 1916 the war was going adversely for England. German machine guns and other advanced weaponry were cutting down the flower of Europe's manhood. England was desperate to find a rapid method of manufacturing TNT and a smokeless gunpowder. A brilliant Jew named Chaim Weizmann invented such a formula that made possible the rapid production of these vital materials, thus changing the course of the war. In return, Lloyd George, representing the British government, told Dr. Weizmann to name his reward. Rejecting personal reward, he requested that Palestine be declared the national homeland for the Jewish people. Consequently the Balfour Declaration was drawn up and signed on November 2, 1917.

> *Dear Lord Rothchild:*
> *I have much pleasure in conveying to you, on behalf of his Majesty's Government, the following declaration of sympathy with Jewish Zionist aspirations, which has been submitted to, and approved by, the Cabinet. His Majesty's Government views with favor the establishment in Palestine of a national home for the Jewish people, and will use their best endeavors to facilitate the achievement of this object, it being clearly understood that nothing shall be done which may prejudice the civil and religious rights of existing non-Jewish communities in Palestine, or the rights and political status enjoyed by Jews in any other country.*
> *I should be grateful if you would bring this declaration to the knowledge of the Zionist Federation.*
>
> > *Yours sincerely,*
> > *Arthur James Balfour*

Could it be a coincidence of language that the impetus to officially start the regathering of Israel was prophesied as a "noise and shaking" and that the fulfillment took place during the world's loudest war over TNT and gunpowder? I heard enough TNT exploded after World War II while stationed in Germany to know that it is always associated with a great shaking. Fearing our former Russian "allies" would sweep down into Germany and confiscate our stockpiles of P-51, P-47, and P-38 aircraft, the U.S. government ordered demolition crews to destroy them. For two months our air base was "shaken" by the detonation of TNT as those once-mighty fighter planes were destroyed. It is not necessary to be dogmatic on this point, but the parallel between dynamite and a "noise" and a "shaking" does seem noteworthy.

The gathering back of the Jews into the land of Palestine after the signing of the Balfour Treaty was indeed a very gradual development ("bone to his bone"). In 1917 it is estimated that there were less than 25,000 Jews in the land. By 1922 there were 83,000; by 1932 — 180,000; by 1935 — 300,000; by 1937 — 430,000; and by 1945 more than 500,000. Today the population is more than 4 million. Between 1917 and 1948, slowly but certainly, "bone came to his bone."

This gradual development of the young nation was not without struggle and trial. In the early days the Jews purchased with Zionist funds 350,000 acres of land, primarily for agricultural purposes. That God blessed this movement seems to be indicated by the amazing increase in rainfall throughout Palestine that anointed the toil of the Jews and produced crops of astounding proportions. When I was in Israel I saw fruit and vegetables larger than those grown in the famed Imperial Valley of California.

While God blessed Israel, Britain reneged on her 1917 treaty and in 1939, after much deliberation over the growing conflicts between the Arabs and the Jews, she issued a White Paper that favored Arab independence and control of the area. After failing to keep peace between the Arabs and the Jews following World War II, the British withdrew from Palestine; shortly thereafter the National Council and the General Zionist Council proclaimed from Tel Aviv the establishment of the Sovereign State of Israel. David Ben Gurion was appointed prime minister and Dr. Chaim Weizmann was elected president of a provisional council. Both the United States and Russia recognized the new nation which, after much debate, was accepted as a member nation into the United Nations by a vote of 37–12.

The gradual development of the reborn nation can be clarified by an examination of the maps on pages 52 and 53 that show the widening occupation of land by Israel.

THE NEW TEMPLE

The hands on Israel's prophecy clock leaped forward on June 8, 1967, when the Israeli troops marched into the Old City of Jerusalem and took it with little or no destruction. For the first time in twenty-five hundred years the Jews had gained complete control over the most important area in the entire world. Suddenly the world was aware of what Bible teachers have been saying for centuries, that Mount Moriah, the site of the Temple of Jesus' day, was to the Jews the most coveted ground in the world. For the first time in nineteen centuries Israel controlled the site of the old — and new — temple!

The deep significance of the 1967 Six-Day War is seen in the prospect that at long last Israel can rebuild its temple. This is not just a national yearning but a prophetic requirement of God's Word. There are six biblical passages that require the rebuilding of the temple in the last days.

> *And he shall confirm the covenant with many for one week; and in the midst of the week he shall cause the sacrifice and the oblation to cease, and for the overspreading of abominations he shall make it desolate, even until the consummation, and that determined shall be poured upon the desolate. (Daniel 9:27)*

> *And from the time that the daily sacrifice shall be taken away, and the abomination that maketh desolate set up, there shall be a thousand two hundred and ninety days. (Daniel 12:11)*

When ye, therefore, shall see the abomination of desolation, spoken of by Daniel the prophet, stand in the holy place (whoso readeth, let him understand). (Matthew 24:15)

But when ye shall see the abomination of desolation, spoken of by Daniel, the prophet, standing where it ought not (let him that readeth understand), then let them that be in Judaea flee to the mountains. (Mark 13:14)

Let no man deceive you by any means; for that day shall not come, except there come a falling away first, and that man of sin be revealed, the son of perdition, who opposeth and exalteth himself above all that is called God, or that is worshiped, so that he, as God, sitteth in the temple of God, showing himself that he is God. (2 Thessalonians 2:3-4)

And there was given me a reed unto like a rod; and the angel stood, saying: Rise, and measure the temple of God, and the altar, and them that worship therein. But the court, which is without the temple, leave out, and measure it not; for it is given unto the Gentiles, and the holy city shall they tread under foot forty and two months. (Revelation 11:1-2)

These verses predict that in the middle of the seven-year tribulation period the Antichrist will desecrate the temple of God. There is only one spot of ground in all the world so designated — the spot where Solomon built the first temple, where the Jews built the second temple after the Babylonian captivity, and where Herod refurbished the temple of Jesus' day. As we have seen, this temple was destroyed in A.D. 70. Ever since the Jews were driven out of the land by the Romans in the second cenury after Christ, it has been impossible for them to rebuild the temple.

Obviously, for the temple to be destroyed in the future it must first be rebuilt. The obstacles to rebuilding the temple in Jerusalem seem insurmountable! The Muslims' multimillion-dollar Dome of the Rock is located on the spot where the temple should be. The Arab countries threaten war. Most Jews profess disinterest, the new government of Jerusalem has guaranteed protection to all existing holy sites, and world opinion seems opposed to the idea. But of this you can be certain—

1946 — At this time Jews and Arabs were living together in cities throughout Palestine. Immigration of more Jews was forbidden by the British.

1947 — After the British withdrawal, hostilities erupted between the Arabs and Jews. The U.N. partitioned the country and sought to keep the peace.

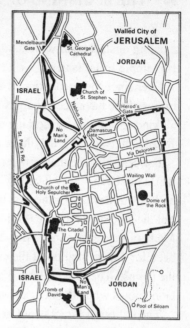

1949 — Following the war for independence, Israel increased her possession of key areas. The U.N. patroled a "no man's land" that provided a buffer area between the land held by Israel and that of the Arabs. It was not an especially successful policy, since hostilities and attacks recurred.

1949-1967 — The Jews were particularly irritated by laws forbidding their entrance into the Holy City. Two Jerusalems grew up during this time: New Jerusalem, owned by the Israelis, and the old city controlled by Jordan. The temple area was possessed by the Arabs.

1967 — The Six-Day War ended with further substantial acquisitions by Israel. In spite of threats by many world powers and the Arab nations, Israel retained these additions of these lands. Most important of all their 1967 gains was the old walled city of Jerusalem. For the first time in 1900 years the Holy City is in the hands of Jews. This is one of the most prophetically strategic events in the last half century— just 50 years after World War I.

existing obstacles notwithstanding—there will be a third Jewish temple in Jerusalem!

Ever since the occupation of the city of Jerusalem by Israeli troops, there have been charges and countercharges, stories and all kinds of rumors concerning the rebuilding of the temple of Jerusalem. Naturally, they have all been officially denied.

For centuries the daily prayer of faithful Jews all over the world has been, "May it be thy will that the temple be speedily built in our days." For the first time in 1,897 years the Jews control the land on which the third temple will some day be built. Many of the Jews' earnest prayers at the Wailing Wall have been for the occupation of the city and the reestablishment of the temple. The first of these prayers has been answered. Only God knows when the next answer will come to pass.

The nation of Israel is not nearly as united internally as most Gentiles seem to think. There are serious differences between the Zionist politicians and the Orthodox Jewish leaders. Zionism is a nationalistic movement, and many of its leaders, including Theodore Hertzel, its founder, have been atheists. Orthodox Jews, however, have migrated to this land to fulfill their supreme religious interests. New reports from Israel frequently reveal these conflicts.

In August 1967 Colonel Shlomo Goren, chief chaplain of the Israeli Army, led a group of fifty worshipers into the Harem Al-Sharif Mosque courtyard for a special prayer meeting. He announced that a prayer service would be held in the shadow of this Muslim shrine. He then announced his intention of doing the same thing the following week. Immediately Colonel Goren was publicly rebuked and contradicted in the Jerusalem press. In short order the Chief Rabbinate of Israel printed a large notice warning that "entrance to the area is forbidden by Jewish law." The *Jerusalem Post* quickly informed the world that "the temple is

not the army's business and it cannot be the business of the
army's chief chaplain. It thus becomes the army's business
to step in and define the proper activities of its own highest
religious representative before grave damage is done." He
was ordered by General Moshe Dayan, the minister of
defense, to "cease and desist. We have enough trouble with
the Arabs without stirring up a holy war with the entire
Muslim world over Mount Moriah."[2] Twenty-four hours
later Colonel Goren cancelled his plan for the prayer meeting the following week and has not been known to return to
that site for such purposes.

Indications from sympathetic Jews all over the world suggest that a secret conflict rages on. An unusual seven-by-
eleven inch ad appeared in the *Washington Post* on May 21,
1967, as follows:

To Persons of the Jewish Faith All Over the World

*The project to rebuild the temple of God in Israel is
now being started. With divine guidance and hope the
temple will be completed. It will signal a new era in
Judaism. Jews will be inspired to conduct themselves
in such a moral way that our Maker will see fit to pay
us a visit here on earth.*

*Imagine the warm feeling that will be ours when
this happy event will take place. This Is My God, by
Herman Wouk, is the book that was the inspiration for
this understanding. God will place in the minds of many
persons in all walks of Jewish life the desire to participate in this work. Executive talents, administrators, and
workers in all levels are needed. All efforts will be anon-
ymous. God will know those desiring to participate.*

GOD'S WILL SHALL PREVAIL

The sponsor of this ad is not publicly known, but it is strange indeed that two weeks later Jerusalem was conquered by Israeli troops!

In fairness to the Israeli government, it should be pointed out that they have made every effort to restrain Jewish enthusiasts who seek to rebuild the temple. Government leaders are well aware of the fact that one of their great assets in fighting against the Arabs has been the natural disunity of the Arab nations. But there is no other single factor so likely to unite the Arabs in starting a holy war as the destruction of the Dome of the Rock or the occupation by Jews of Harem Al-Sharif. Israeli officials are well aware of their numerical inferiority when comparing their meager population of 2 million against 54 million Arab neighbors, almost all of whom are Muslims.

Ever since the Israeli troops occupied the city of Jerusalem, a rash of rumors about supposed plans for the rebuilding of the temple has appeared, almost all of which have proved false. The most notable was in August 1967 when Christians saw the following report in the British magazine, *The Christian and Christianity Today:*

> *Five hundred rail-car loads of stone from Bedford, considered to be among the finest building stone in the world, are being freighted pre-cut to exact specifications, and one consignment has already been dispatched to Israel. Shipments are being handled by Pier 26 in New York.*
>
> *This report, received from authoritative sources in Sellersburg, Indiana, said cornerstones for the third Jerusalem temple are already in Israel. Materials for this temple have been secretly in preparation for seven years, the report went on, and it is believed American*

*Jews are mainly responsible for financially undergirding
the whole project.*

*Strong rumors from other usually reliable circles say
the two freestanding pillars for the new temple have
already been cast in bronze. If the pattern of Solomon's
Temple is followed, the twin hollow columns may be
named Jachin and Boaz. The meaning of these names,
"Jehovah will establish" and "In him is strength," symbolize the continuity and power of the Davidic dynasty
founded upon God's great covenant with David (2 Samuel
7:8-17).*

This report was reproduced in many Christian periodicals,
and by September 1967 the Bedford, Indiana, Chamber
of Commerce was deluged with letters, telegrams, telephone
calls, and visitors from all over the world. The following
is the reproduction of the answer I received from their
secretary.

December 18, 1967

*Yours is one of a number of inquiries about reported
shipments of Indiana limestone to be used in rebuilding
the temple. The Indiana Limestone Institute, representing
most of the stone companies, has checked this report and
we find no foundation for the report—unless the stone
has been ordered under some surreptitious means. Of
course, with many thousands of tons being shipped
weekly to markets such as New York, we have no way of
determining the ultimate destination of every order.*

*Betty Pace
Office Secretary*

My own investigation of this report proved as fruitless as others. A former church member now living in New York City could find no evidence of such massive stone movements as suggested by the British periodical. I was able to make contact with two residents in the Bedford area, and although at first both seemed to promise some confirmation of the article, further investigation only revealed that Bedford, Indiana, limestone is similar to Jerusalem limestone, and stones large enough for such a project are cut there for export all over the world.

A quarry owner did inform me that one of the large stone quarries in Bedford had recently been sold to a group of three New York Jews. A spokesman for this firm vehemently denies any knowledge of such a shipment. Even if the rumor had any foundation, we would not expect those who have anything to do with the project to admit it. When the time comes for such rebuilding, we can be almost certain that it will be done secretly unless some unforeseen compromise with the Arabs can be worked out. The only significant information gleaned from my investigation was that Jewish stone masons from Israel had been brought to Bedford to study the use of pneumatic equipment and other high speed devices for stone cutting. This would not, of course, be limited to temple construction, since Jerusalem limestone is the major building material throughout Israel.

Theologically speaking, the publicized Israeli position is that "the restoration of the temple will have to wait until the coming of the Messiah." However, it cannot be denied that the great Jewish philosopher of the Middle Ages, Maimonides, contended that it was the responsibility of every generation of Jews to rebuild the temple if the site was retaken. This attitude is expressed by the Israeli historian Eldad, as quoted in *Time* magazine, June 30, 1967: "We are at the stage where David was when he liberated Jerusalem. From that time until the construction of the temple by Solomon only one generation passed. So will it be with us."

The big problem is the multimillion-dollar mosque, the Dome of the Rock, sitting on the place of the ancient temple sacrifice. Some have tried to suggest that perhaps this location is not the only place in Jerusalem the temple could be built, and thus the Muslim mosque and the Jewish temple could coexist. No careful Bible student would accept that reasoning. Araunah's threshing floor, purchased by David, was the original site of Solomon's temple. There is no substitute on the face of the earth for that spot. But what will happen to the present structure? Historian Eldad, again quoted in the *Time* magazine article, may express the feeling of many Jews. He said, "It is, of course, an open question. Who knows? Perhaps there will be an earthquake."

Prophetically speaking, there can be no question that the temple will be rebuilt! What is of critical concern to us is that after nineteen centuries the events of the last few years have thrust a temple into the realm of probability. Perhaps, as Eldad said, there may be an earthquake, planned or otherwise. Perhaps unimaginable events will result in an agreement with the Arabs for the purchase of their mosque, although that seems unlikely.

It is not unthinkable to suggest when the United Nations' "peacekeeping force" establishes a government that they can control in Iraq and Kuwait that they will develop a resettlement plan for the PLO. By moving them to Kuwait or Saudi Arabia or Jordan, they could, with oil money, be set up in far better living conditions than they have today. And as part of the agreement, they may dismantle the Dome of the Rock and move it to Babylon, the new capital of the world. For this, the rich Jews of the world could be counted on for financing.

Or it may be that not until the Antichrist comes and makes

a covenant with Israel will they be permitted to rebuild their temple. As far as we know, nothing requires that it be rebuilt before the Tribulation begins, and certainly the first three and one-half years is ample time to do it.

BONES AND BREATH

From the early days of the regathering, as the bones of the vision came together, Zionists had limited organizational unity. But gradually this governmental "sinew" and "flesh" was prepared for the "skin" of the self-government, which was fully established on May 14, 1948, when Israel declared her independence. All that is left of the prophet's vision to be fulfilled relates to the statement: "But there was no breath in them." That expression is not difficult for Bible students to decipher, since "breath" or "wind" used symbolically often refers to the Holy Spirit. That would indicate that Israel is going to have a fresh visitation of the Holy Spirit or a revival one of these days. That is certainly in agreement with many other passages that predict a great spiritual awakening when the Jews call upon the Messiah they rejected in A.D. 30 (see Joel 2:18-32; Revelation 7:1-9).

The revival pictured here is the only part of this entire prophecy that has not yet been fulfilled. Over four decades have passed since Israel became a nation, and the Jews as a nation still reject Christ as their Messiah. That is the reason the prophet challenged them to "hear the word of the Lord" (Ezekiel 37:4). For the Scriptures testify of the true identity of the Messiah; if they would genuinely "hear," they would be forced to recognize Christ as their Lord.

The last time I was in Israel, one of the Jewish guides informed us that the national sport in their young country was "Bible quiz contests." Next to military heroes, the outstanding

citizen each year was the National Quiz Leader. Without real-
izing it, the Jews are sowing in the minds of their youth the
seeds of the "word of the Lord." When the day comes for the
Spirit of God to "breathe upon those," a mighty revival will
break out and turn millions of Jews to Christ. Then, as the
prophet said, they will live. Jesus Christ is the source of life.
Only he can raise the dead, whether spiritual or physical, for
only he has "the words of eternal life" (John 6:68). Like the
Gentiles, when Jews reverse their opinion of Jesus Christ and
accept him as Lord and Savior, they receive eternal life.

Truly these are thrilling days, when so many long-prophe-
sied events enter the realm of possibility at the same time —
particularly when they stem from the first sign of World War I
as predicted by our Lord. Certainly it should make Christians
vitally concerned about living so as to be prepared when the
Lord comes for his Church.

1. David L. Cooper, quoted in *The World's Greatest Library.*
2. Leo Herman, Copley News Service, April 28, 1968.

FIVE
RUSSIA AND THE MID EAST

During World War I Kaiser Wilhelm gave permission for
Leon Trotsky, the Russian exile, and his group of revolutionar-
ies to travel across Germany in a sealed boxcar. The German
leader expected these Marxists to sabotage the Russian army
on his eastern front. Little did he dream that they would overthrow the Czarist government and then conquer Germany
only a generation later. He was equally unaware that his order
would help to fulfill Bible prophecy. For the prophet Ezekiel,
twenty-five hundred years before, had predicted that Russia
would become a major power during the end time. When the
prophet made his prediction, Russia was on the fringe of civilization. In fact, the present capital of Russia had only twelve
hundred residents in A.D. 1000. What makes this prediction so
interesting is that World War I, the great sign of the Lord's
return, enabled Communists to turn the toothless bear into a
vicious monster.

The first attempt by socialists to overthrow the czar in 1905
failed despite popular opposition to the Russo-Japanese War.
However, in 1917, after Russia had suffered through three

years of battle against Germany, the people were sufficiently demoralized so that false propaganda, revolutionary tactics, and spies in the communication media enabled the Communists to ruthlessly overthrow the czar and murder the entire Romanov family.

The prophecy of Ezekiel 38 and 39 affords us one of the most important predictions relating to Russia and our day. It reads almost like a daily newspaper, and stands as a monument to the accuracy of the prophetic Word of God. When I first started preaching on prophecy and predicted, on the basis of this text, that Russia would go down against Israel some day, people laughed. Today no one laughs at the possibility, for it seems only a question of time. It would be helpful for the reader to pause here and read these two chapters before proceeding. You will be amazed to see how easy it is to understand the events which are forecast. Furthermore, you will be able to visualize a stormy and tragic time ahead for the little nation of Israel.

The participants in this dramatic conflict are so clearly described in Ezekiel's prophecy that we can positively identify them. Russia and her chief leader are unquestionably the planners of an imminent attack against Israel, and we can also identify most of the allies on both sides. There are three signs marking Russia as the protagonist in this drama: the etymology of the names; the antireligious character of the nation; and its geographical location.

The nouns identifying the invading nation in this war have been held for years to be Russia, "Rosh" or "Gog"; Moscow, "Meshech"; and Tobolsk, "Tubal," the largest state.

"Son of man, set thy face against Gog, of the land of Magog, the chief prince Of Meshech and Tubal, and prophesy against him" (Ezekiel 38:2).

Genesis, chapter 10, is of great help in establishing the identity of these peoples. Magog was the second son of Japheth who, according to Josephus, the great historian, settled north of the Black Sea. Tubal and Meshech were the fifth and sixth sons of Japheth, whose descendants settled south of the Black Sea. It is believed that these people intermarried and became known as Magog, the dominant tribe. The name *Moscow* comes from the tribal name Meshech, and Tobolsk, the name of the principal state, comes from Tubal. The noun *Gog* is from the original tribal name, Magog, which gradually became *Rosh*, then *Rus*, and today is known as Russia. In the very interesting book *The Late Great Planet Earth*, my friend Hal Lindsey presents a lengthy discussion of the identity of these nations. I was so impressed by the accuracy of his sources and his readable style that I obtained permission to quote him at length, with numbered footnotes indicating his sources.[1]

DEAD MEN DO TELL TALES!

"It is necessary on the next few pages to establish some documentation from ancient history. Some people find this subject a little dull, to say the least. If this is your case, you may wish to skim over the high points. For others, it will prove to be rewarding to check carefully the grounds upon which the historical case is built.

"Herodotus, the fifth-century B.C. Greek philosopher, is quoted as mentioning Meshech and Tubal. He identified them with a people named the Samaritans and Muschovites who lived at that time in the ancient province of Pontus in northern Asia Minor.[2]

"Josephus, a Jewish historian of the first century, says that the people of his day known as the Moschevi and Thobelites were founded by Meshech and Tubal, respectively. He said, 'Magog is called the Scythians by the Greeks.' He continued by saying that these people lived in the northern regions above the Caucasus Mountains.[3]

"Pliny, a noted Roman writer of early Christian times, said, 'Hierapolis, taken by the Scythians, was afterward called Magog.'[4] In this he shows that the dreaded barbaric people called the Scythians were identified with their ancient tribal name. Any good history book of ancient times traces the Scythians to be a principal part of the people who make up modern Russia.

"Wilhelm Gesenius, a great Hebrew scholar of the early nineteenth century, discusses these words in his unsurpassed *Hebrew and English Lexicon.* 'Meshech,' he says, 'was founder of the Moschi, a barbarous people, who dwelt in the Moschian mountains.'[5]

"This scholar went on to say that the Greek name, 'Moschi,' derived from the Hebrew name Meshech, is the source of the name for the city of Moscow. In discussing Tubal he said, 'Tubal is the son of Rapheth, founder of the Tibereni, a people dwelling on the Black Sea to the west of the Moschi.'

"Gesenius concludes by saying that these people undoubtedly make up the modern Russian people.

"There is one more name to consider in this line of evidence. It is the Hebrew word, 'Rosh,' translated 'chief' in Ezekiel 38:2, 3 of the King James and Revised Standard Versions. The word literally means in Hebrew the 'top' or 'head' of something. According to most scholars, this word is used in the sense of a proper name, not as a descriptive noun qualifying the word 'prince.'

"The German scholar, C. F. Keil, says after a careful grammatical analysis that it should be translated as a proper name, i.e., Rosh. He says, 'The Byzantine and Arabic writers frequently mention a people called Ros and Rus, dwelling in the country of Taurus, and reckoned among the Scythian tribes.'[6]

"Dr. Gesenius in his *Hebrew Lexicon* says, 'Rosh was a designation for the tribes then north of the Taurus Mountains, dwelling in the neighborhood of the Volga.'[7] He concluded that in this name and tribe we have the first historical trace of the Russ or Russian nation.

"In the light of the abundant evidence, it is no wonder that men foresaw Russia's role in history power. Bishop Lowth of England was one of these men. He wrote in 1710: 'Rosh, taken as a proper name, in Ezekiel signifies the inhabitants of Scythia, from whom the modern Russians derive their name.'"[8]

RUSSIA'S ATHEISM

The evidence for the identity of Russia as the principal nation in this prophecy does not rest solely on etymology. We must likewise consider the matter of their religious philosophy, implied by Ezekiel 38:3.

"And say: Thus saith the Lord God: Behold, I am against thee, O Gog, the chief prince of Meshech and Tubal."

Discerning Bible students quickly notice this unusual statement. God so consistently favors mankind that this kind of judgment rarely appears. Our God is such a God of love that he preeminently seeks to help humanity, and through the gift of his Son he has forever established the fact that he is *for* man. Scripture teaches that it is not God's will "that any should perish, but that all should come to repentance" (2 Peter 3:9). The Lord Jesus said of little children, "Neither is it the will of your father which is in heaven that one of these little ones should perish" (Matthew 18:14). This, plus the story of the prodigal son given by Jesus Christ himself, shows that God is for us (Luke 15:11-32).

Since therefore God has established a long history of being for mankind, only one reason may be given why he is pictured here as saying, "I am against thee, O Gog," namely, Russia's atheism. God is only against those nations that are against him, and even then he does not turn on them suddenly, but after a protracted period of antagonism against his will. History shows that atheistic communism emanates from the political leadership in Russia and extends throughout their nefarious system all over the world. No nation in the history of the world has destroyed more flesh than Russia through the spread of communism. This is true in her own land as well as in China, the eastern European satellite nations, Africa (particularly in the Congo and Biafra), India, Indonesia, and many other places.

But her greatest sin has not been the destruction of flesh, as serious as that is. Her greatest sin has been the soul damnation caused by her atheistic ideology. This has been accomplished not only through Communist leaders in Communist countries, but through Communist infiltrators and dupes on university campuses of the free world. The Lord Jesus Christ's indictment of the Pharisees in Matthew 23 reveals the attitude of God toward the destroyers of men's souls — and it reveals his attitude toward Russia. Certainly no nation has done more to destroy faith in God than Communist Russia, thereby earning the enmity of God.

Another factor that evokes the wrath of God against Russia and her leaders is their mistreatment of the Jews. This will be discussed in detail later, but it is enough to say here that Russia stands second only to Adolf Hitler in cruelty to Jews.

It was not until the early 1990s that pressure from the United States and the near collapse of their entire economic system, food delivery system, and the movement to democracy by their Eastern European satellites that Mikhail Gorbachev gave his endorsement to the resettlement of 500,000 Soviet Jews to the Holy Land. This order was not given in obedience to God or an expression of humanitarianism to Israel or even in response to the demands of the United States. It was an economic necessity due to the unrealistically stifling system of government controlled economy. God has already proclaimed that Israel is his delight, that "I am against them that are against thee." Therefore it is clear why Russia qualifies for the indictment: "I am against thee, O Gog."

RUSSIA'S LOCATION

The third and most significant reason for dogmatically identifying "Rosh" or the land of Magog, Meshech, and Tubal as Russia is its geographical location. When the Bible gives geographical directions, it lists them in relation to Israel. When the writer says "south," it means south of Palestine; if he indicates "east," it means east of Palestine. Consequently, when we see "uttermost parts of the north," Ezekiel 38:15 and 39:2 (RSV), it is clear that this nation could only be Russia. In order to verify this we need only to take a world map or globe and draw a line straight north from Israel. The entire "uttermost parts of the north" is covered by the USSR.

When all three of these factors are taken into consideration, the only nation in the history of the world that comes close to fulfilling the description is Russia, one of the dominant nations on the globe today.

Verification that this prophecy is on the verge of fulfillment can be obtained when we notice that.

According to Ezekiel 38:5-6, Gog's confederates are among the current friends of Russia. Those not presently within her circle are being lured into her orbit of influence. Turning again to Hal Lindsey's book for a quotation on the identity of Russia's allies, we find some very interesting information.

PERSIA

"All authorities agree on who Persia is today. It is modern
Iran. This is significant because it is being wooed to join the
United Arab Republic in its hostility against Israel. The Russians are at this moment seeking to gain footholds in Iran by
various overtures of aid. In order to mount the large-scale
invasion predicted by Ezekiel, Russia would need Iran as an
ally. It would be much more difficult to move a large land
army across the Caucasus Mountains that border Turkey than
the Elburz Mountains that border Iran. Iran's general terrain is
also much easier to cross than Turkey's. Transportation, however, will be needed through both countries."

It is quite evident to anyone who is watching the Soviet
Union closely that even though they made a perfunctory effort
to show the allies their support, the truth is, they still regard
the Iraqi government as friends. They were the principal supplier of their over $180 billion arms buildup prior to the 1991
war for Kuwait and have not abandoned their relationship
with them. Secret intelligence suggested that Russian advisers
remained in Iraq all during the war in the Gulf and that the
Soviets supplied them with strategic spare parts — contrary to
their public denunciations of Saddam Hussein. We will see in
this chapter that Arab nations will, in the near future, yet be
allied with Russia against Israel.

ETHIOPIA OR CUSH

"Ethiopia is a translation of the Hebrew word, Cush. Cush
was the first son of Ham, one of the sons of Noah.

"Moses mentions 'the land of Cush' as originally being
adjacent to an area near the Tigris and Euphrates rivers
(Genesis 2:13).

"After examining many authorities on the subject, the

writer discovered once again why Dr. Gesenius is recognized
as one of the great scholars of history. Gesenius summarized
all of the evidence as follows: (1) The Cushites were black
men; (2) they migrated first to the Arabian peninsula and then
across the Red Sea to the area south of Egypt; (3) all the black
people of Africa are descended from Cush.[9]

"Cush is translated 'Ethiopia' twenty-one times in the King
James Version, which is somewhat misleading. It is certain
that the ancient Ethiopians (modern Abyssinia) are made up of
Cushites, but they do not represent all of them, according to
history.

"The sobering conclusion is this: many of the African
nations will be united and allied with the Russians in the invasion of Israel. This is in accord with Daniel's graphic description of this invasion (11:36-45). Here the Russian force is
called 'the king of the north' and the African (Cush) is called
'the king of the south.'

"One of the most active areas for the Communist 'gospel' is
in Africa. As we see further developments in this area in the
future, we realize that it will become converted to communism."

LIBYA OR PUT

"Libya is the translation of the original Hebrew word *Put.*
We have the same problem pinpointing these people as with
Cush. Put was the third son of Ham (Genesis 10:6). The
descendants of Put migrated to the land west of Egypt and
became the source of the North African Arab nations, such as
Libya, Algeria, Tunisia, and Morocco. The first settlement of
Put was called Libya by the ancient historian, Josephus, and
Pliny.[10] The Greek translation of the Hebrew Old Testament,
called the Septuagint, translates Put as Libya in about 165 B.C.

"The conclusion is that Russia's ally, Put, certainly included more than what is now called Libya. Once again there are current events to show the beginning of this alliance.

"The territory of Northern Africa is becoming solidly pro-Soviet.[11] Algeria appears to be already Communist and allied with Russia.

"As we watch this area in the next few years we shall see indications that it is destined to join the southern sphere of power which will attack Israel along with the 'king of the north.'"

GOMER AND ITS HORDES

"Gomer was the eldest son of Japheth and the father of Ashkenaz, Riphath, and Togarmah. These people make up an extremely important part of the future Russian invasion force.

"Dr. Young, citing the best of the most recent archeological finds, says of Gomer and his hordes: 'They settled on the north of the Black Sea, and then spread themselves southward and westward to the extremities of Europe.'[12]

"Gesenius speaks of part of Gomer's 'hordes' as being Ashkenaz, 'the proper name of a region and a nation in northern Asia, sprung from the Cimmerians who are the ancient people of Gomer. The modern Jews understand it to be Germany, and call that country by this Hebrew name. . . .'[13]

"Josephus called the sons of Ashkenaz 'the Rheginians,' and a map of the ancient Roman Empire places them in the area of modern Poland, Czechoslovakia, and eastern Germany to the banks of the Danube River. The modern Jewish Talmud confirms the same geographical picture.

"The conclusion is that Gomer and its hordes are a part of the vast area of modern eastern Europe, including eastern Germany and the Slovak countries."

TOGARMAH AND ITS HORDES

"In Ezekiel 38:6 the house of Togarmah, and all its hordes are specifically pointed out as being from the uttermost north. Gesenius says that 'they are a northern nation and country sprung from Gomer abounding in horses and mules.' Some of the sons of Togarmah founded Armenia, according to their own claim today, Gesenius continued.

"Dr. Bauman traces evidence of some of the sons of Togarmah to the Turkoman tribes in central Asia. This would explain the phrase: of the uttermost north, and all its hordes.

"The conclusion is that Togarmah is part of modern southern Russia and is probably the home of the Cossacks and other people of the eastern part of Russia. It is interesting to note that the Cossacks have always loved horses and have been recognized as producing the finest army of cavalry in the world. Today they are reported to have several divisions of cavalry. It is believed by some military men that cavalry will actually be used in the invasion of the Middle East just as Ezekiel and other prophets described it. During the Korean War the Red Chinese proved that horses are still the fastest means of moving a large attacking force into battle zones. Isn't it a coincidence that such terrain stands between Russia and the Israeli?

"Ezekiel indicates that he hasn't given a complete list of allies. Enough is given, however, to amaze us with the number of people and nations which will be involved."

COMMAND TO GOG

"Ezekiel, prophetically addressing the Russian ruler, commands him to 'be prepared; yes, prepare yourself, you and all your companies that are assembled about you, and you be a guard and a commander for them' (Ezekiel 38:7, AMP). In other words, the Russian ruler is to equip his confederates with arms and to assume command.

"Any who doubt the interpretations of this chapter may understandably be unnerved by the realization that almost all the countries cited as part of this great army are today looking to Russia for weapons of war!

"We have seen that Russia will arm and equip a vast confederacy. This powerful group of allies will lead an attack on restored Israel. However, Russia and her confederates will be destroyed completely by an act that Israel will recognize as being from God. This stunning deliverance will bring many in Israel to believe in their true Messiah (Ezekiel 38:15 ff.)."[14]

From all this we learn that a dominant leader in Russia called Gog and described as the "chief prince of Rosh" is going to arise and lead Russia into a vast northeastern confederation of nations including Iran, Ethiopia, and other African nations, Germany, Armenia, possibly the Turks, conceivably some Orientals, and whoever else can be included with the statement, "And many peoples with thee." This group of evil nations, headed by Russia, make up a massive northeastern confederation that will advance against Israel in the last days.

RUSSIA'S OPPONENTS

Before examining their invasion tactics, we should glimpse the identity of the opponents of Russia and her northeastern confederacy. They are described in Ezekiel 38:13 as "Sheba, and Dedan, and the merchants of Tarshish, with all the young lions thereof." Of all the nations mentioned in this chapter, the descendants of Sheba and Dedan are the most difficult to trace, primarily because of the mixing of the races that existed for centuries in the Middle East. Another factor that makes it difficult concerns two sets of sons named Sheba and Dedan.

In Genesis 10:7 we note one set was born to Ramah, the son of Cush. Another set was born to Abraham's son Jokshan whose mother was Keturah (Genesis 25:3), whom he married after the death of Sarah. Which of these tribal groups Ezekiel had in mind is not clear.

It is not quite so difficult to establish the identity of Tarshish, which is referred to many times in Scripture as a seafaring nation or a nation of ships. Most Bible scholars have identified England as the nation of Tarshish because of her longstanding interest in sea power. The fact that her power on the ocean has declined since World War II so that she is a fifth-rate power today is not incompatible with this prophecy. The "young lions" seem to belong to Tarshish and could be the only reference to the United States, Canada, and Australia to be found in Scripture. The Bible frequently uses animals symbolically to depict governments. For example, Daniel 7 portrays Babylon as a lion, Medo-Persia as a bear, Greece as a leopard, etc. Here the reference to "young lions" would indicate young nations that were the original cubs of Tarshish or England. Therefore, we may reasonably conclude that the western democracies that primarily stem from England are represented by Ezekiel 38:13. That the position of prominence has passed from Tarshish to one of the young lions would not negate this possibility. In fact, as we shall see, the predicted diplomatic action seems to be the style used by western democracies today.

TARGET: ISRAEL

Of all the participants in this global drama, the easiest to identify is the intended victim, Israel. The vision of the valley of dry bones in Ezekiel 37, presenting a picture of the regathering of Israel into Palestine, is the prophecy immediately preceding this one, which shows Israel as the target of

Russia and her northeastern confederation. Ezekiel 38:8 makes her identity particularly clear.

> *After many days thou shalt be visited; in the latter years thou shalt come into the land that is brought back from the sword, and is gathered out of many people, against the mountains of Israel, which have been always waste; but it is brought forth out of the nations, and they shall dwell safely, all of them.*

Another identifying expression is found in verse 16, "And thou shalt come up against my people of Israel, as a cloud to cover the land." See also 39:4, 7, 9, and 11-16. There can be no doubt that the little nation of Israel will be the target of the northeastern confederacy in the last days. Fifteen or twenty years ago skeptics and doubters ridiculed the Bible for making such a suggestion. Today they read about it in the daily newspaper, most of the time on the front page.

COMMUNISM IS NOT DEAD!

One of the biggest hoaxes about communism in the early years of the 1990s is that it is dying. It is reorganizing on a grand scale — but out of necessity, not out of a new wave of humanitarianism! "Glasnost" and "Peristroika" have permitted some changes in the Soviet Union that sparked even more of a craving for "democracy" than the Communist lords of the Kremlin had anticipated. They desperately needed Western loans, capital investments, and grain subsidies — all of which they have now received. The "restructuring" within the Soviet Union is not to be confused with democracy as we know it in the West. It is a tactic to lull the West into making concessions and the time has come to move heavily back into totalitarian control.

Even as President George Bush ram-rodded through the United States Congress a one billion dollar grain subsidy to the Soviets, which many considered a subtle bribe to secure Soviet approval of the Allied attack on Saddam Hussein for invading Kuwait, the Soviets never sent troops or armament, but continued to spend 25 percent of their annual budget on war materials. State-of-the-art tanks rolled off their assembly plants at the rate of three per week, as did their most advanced missiles and MiG-29 aircraft—considered by many to be superior to our latest F-16s. This is hardly the action of a peace-loving superpower interested in bringing "peace on earth" unless you interpret "peace" the way Communists do, meaning that the rest of the world gives up and lets them run "the New World Order."

And before you write that off as more "Communist-phobia," just remember two things: the Communists still control the guns in all the eastern European countries. Soviet troops are still in huge numbers in what was East Germany, and other Soviet-influenced countries (even Nicaragua)—and they have given up neither their world conquest objectives nor the total disregard for human life exhibited by the Chinese Communists during the Tiananmen Square uprising when they ruthlessly decimated their own countrymen whose only crime was wanting to be free. We can expect to see the same action by the Soviet "hardliners" when they either jettison their present leader for one equally repressive as themselves, or force him to be a repressive dictator in order to keep his job.

Saddam Hussein provided the Soviets an ideal opportunity to do what they do so well—take one step backward and then take two steps forward to the accomplishment of their goals while the attention of the world is fixated on other subjects. By refusing to back Hussein, they assured his defeat at the hands of the Americans because he was a loose cannon that even they could not control. By maintaining "neutrality," they got to study our best weapons in action to see how they compared with their own. They also got a chance to study our battle techniques for future reference. Then, when the war was over they tried desperately to use diplomacy to assure that a Communist government would come to power in Iraq, Kuwait, and any other Middle Eastern countries they could influence. Even Saudi Arabia is vulnerable after the Americans return home. Then, instead of the Soviets controlling 15 percent of the world's oil as they do now, they will control 60 percent. And they will be tightly allied with the very Muslim nations that Ezekiel 38 and 39 predict they will be allied with when they go down against Israel.

How long would all this take? Not very long! Peace — or at least the overthrow of Iraq — will probably be achieved before this revised edition is published. Look for a U.N. "peacekeeping force" to be established in the entire Middle East region — all with known or secret Communist leadership. Kuwait could be an ideal place for the PLO to resettle; after all, over 400,000 had voluntarily migrated there before the Iraqi invasion. During that time, Russia and her "hordes" would become heavily allied, and Israel would become a sitting duck. All this could be accomplished in one to three years!

Today Russia and her allies obviously prize Israel, but Ezekiel's prophecy seems to indicate a different development of conflict. Ezekiel 38:4 pictures Russia and her allies armed to the teeth and ready to take on another enemy when God intervenes. For the prophet predicted that God will "turn thee back, and put hooks into thy jaws, and I will bring thee forth, and all thine army, horses, and horsemen, all of them clothed with all sorts of armor, even a great company with bucklers and shields, all of them handling swords."

In verses 8-12 we find: "After many days thou shalt be visited; in the latter years thou shalt come into the land that is brought back from the sword, and is gathered out of many people, against the mountains of Israel, which have been always waste; but it is brought forth out of the nations, and they shall dwell safely, all of them. Thou shalt ascend and come like a storm; thou shalt be like a cloud to cover the land, thou, and all thy bands, and many peoples with thee. Thus saith the Lord God: It shall also come to pass that at the same time shall things come into thy mind, and thou shalt think an evil thought; and thou shalt say: I will go up to the land of unwalled villages; I will go to them who are at rest, that dwell safely, all of them dwelling without walls, and having neither bars nor gates, to take a spoil, and to take a prey; to turn thine hand upon the desolate places that are now inhabited, and upon the people that are gathered out of the nations, who have gotten cattle and goods, who dwell in the midst of the land."

Although we cannot be dogmatic here, it would seem that Russia's northeastern confederacy will one day be strong enough to challenge the western confederacy of nations (verse 13) in open combat. When her final preparations are completed, God will put it in her mind to go instead against the little land of Israel. That is not the way current events have lined up.

When all the facts are taken into consideration, we can reasonably conclude that we are seeing vivid similarities to Ezekiel's prophecy in our day. We can expect the present crisis to be resolved soon and a false period of peace to come to Israel. However, that should not give anyone a feeling of complacency. The thing to keep in focus is that after twenty-five hundred years, this prophecy appears very near fulfillment, and the very nations the Bible predicted will come against Israel in the last days are allied together.

RUSSIA'S INVASION

The prophecy of Russia's coming invasion of Israel is quite specific. In fact, the prophet gives what sounds like a description of a massive airborne invasion. Note the words, "Thou shalt ascend and come like a storm; thou shalt be like a cloud to cover the land."

If you have ever been to Fort Bragg during paratroop maneuvers, you would find verse 9 a very apt description, for certainly they "come like a storm . . . like a cloud to cover the land." Again, we are not being dogmatic, for the text does not demand an airborne invasion, but we point it out as an interesting possibility.

The use of cavalry is almost a thing of the past in warfare except with Russia. The Cossacks still boast of having the finest horseflesh in the world. However, writing twenty-five hundred years ago, Ezekiel used terms meaningful to his people. "Horses, swords, armor, bucklers, and shields" could be symbolic terms of implements of warfare that in our day would represent tanks, M-16s, machine guns, rockets, bazookas, etc. The thing to keep in mind is that Russia, the dominant country in this northeastern confederacy of nations and the supplier of weapons to future invaders of Israel, is today the leading manufacturer of weaponry in the Communist world.

We might do well to pause here and ask the question, "Why would Russia want to go against Israel?" Certainly she does not need Israel's land surface, for Russia is the largest country in the world. What would make Russia single out a little country of some 4 million people as her end-time target? We have already seen that God will "put hooks" in Russia's jaws and turn her around so that she thinks evil thoughts toward Israel. The evil thoughts are clearly defined in verses 12 and 13 as greed. That is, Russia will go up there to "take a spoil, and to take a prey . . . to carry away silver and gold, to take away

cattle and goods, to take a great spoil." The answer is very
clear: Israel is destined to become a very rich nation. We have
all witnessed the fact that wealthy Jews from all over the
world, sympathetic toward Israel, have invested millions of
capital in that country. She is without doubt the economic mar-
vel of the world. Well-substantiated reports indicate that an
extensive engineering study of the mineral resources of the
Dead Sea estimated them to be in the vicinity of $3 trillion at
the beginning of this century. Due to inflation they would be
worth $6–8 trillion today. In addition, she is surrounded by oil-
rich countries. Who knows what success the present Israeli oil
drilling attempts will produce!

While in Israel I spoke to the wife of the superintendent of
a Beaumont, Texas, oil drilling company. She indicated that
her husband was prepared to drive an eight-inch pipe down
ten thousand feet if necessary, for he was convinced that oil
would be found somewhere. Of one thing you can be certain:
the more time that elapses, the richer Israel will become. The
richer she gets, the greater she will appear to the greedy monster of communism. It is not difficult to see Russia attacking
Israel just as the prophet predicted. Besides, what is the most
anti-Semitic nation in the world today? Ever since the days of
Joseph Stalin, when he nationalized communism in Russia by
killing the Jews in the Communist party and persecuting many
others, it has been difficult for Jews to live in Russia. Only
enormous diplomatic pressure from the West has helped thousands to get out. Anyone can see that Russia has no love for
the Jew.

RUSSIA'S COMING DESTRUCTION

The purpose of our study of Ezekiel 38 and 39 is to show the
rise of Russia to a major world power in the last days. Her

antagonism toward Israel is another sign or "birth pain" that the end is approaching. We further wish to establish the fact that Israel first gained world prominence from events arising during World War I, the great sign of the end. Now, rather than leaving questions dangling regarding the outcome of Russia's invasion and the time of this event, we shall examine the rest of Ezekiel's prophecy.

Remember that God said to Russia: "I am against thee, O Gog." It is always fatal to be opposed by God. He plans to bring Russia into his trap in Israel. He may use her hatred of Jews, her need for money or other resources, but God controls the destiny of nations. On this occasion he chooses to make an atheistic nation an object lesson to the world. For he plans to destroy Russia in such a way as to "magnify myself" in the eyes of the nations, that "they shall know that I am the Lord" (Ezekiel 38:23).

A careful reading of these chapters indicates that the Russian-led northeastern confederation moves its troops en masse against Israel. The western democracies (Ezekiel 38:13) send an anemic diplomatic note asking, "Art thou come to take a spoil?" Israel is probably looking to the western powers for protection, but instead she receives "diplomacy." This may indicate that American and allied disarmament leave them only words for defense, or it may mean an estrangement between Israel and the Western powers. In any case, when Israel's existence is jeopardized by Russian armies, no human friends come to her aid; in that moment God dramatically comes to her defense.

"And I will smite thy bow (weapons) out of thy left hand, and will cause thine arrows to fall out of thy right hand; thou shalt fall upon the mountains of Israel, thou, and all thy bands, and the people that is with thee; I will give thee unto the ravenous birds of every sort, and to the beasts of the field to be devoured. Thou shalt fall upon the open field; for I have spoken it, saith the Lord God" (Ezekiel 39:3-5).

Chapter 39 indicates that there will be an earthquake and mighty shaking so great that "mountains shall be thrown down." And beasts and birds of prey will be summoned to clean up the human carnage.

"And ye shall eat fat till ye be full, and drink blood till ye be drunken, of my sacrifice which I have sacrificed for you. Thus ye shall be filled at my table with horses and chariots, with mighty men, and with all men of war, saith the Lord God. And I will set my glory among the nations, and all the nations shall see my judgment that I have executed, and my hand that I have laid upon them. So the house of Israel shall know that I am the Lord, their God, from that day and forward" (Ezekiel 39:19-22).

From this we get a very clear picture that Almighty God is going to destroy Russia's massive armies by his supernatural power. Furthermore, he will send a fire on the homeland of Magog, or Russia. We can conclude then that Russia will be almost entirely destroyed.

"I will send fire on Magog, and on those who dwell securely in the coastlands" (39:6, RSV).

This could mean that the Communist spies who have infiltrated positions of influence in the isles (such as America, Canada, Britain, etc.) will be struck by a ball of fire. From a practical standpoint, the F.B.I. may someday get help from an unexpected source — Almighty God. Suddenly the Communists on the university campus, the security risks in government, and agents hiding elsewhere would die by fire. In one dramatic moment, God will solve the greatest internal threat to the security of the free countries of the world. In addition, the slaves of worldwide communism would suddenly be free. Thus we may see a day when the world will be rid of Communist chains.

But there's no end to this war—man's inhumanity to man will be repeated. Into the void created by the destruction of communism will march the world dictator called the Antichrist. He will bring his own brand of evil but that is a story for another chapter.

A SPIRIT OF REVIVAL

"So will I make my holy name known in the midst of my people, Israel, and I will not let them pollute my holy name any more; and the nations shall know that I am the Lord, the Holy One in Israel" (Ezekiel 39:7).

God's purpose in this is to make known the glory of his name throughout Israel. Certainly they do not know him today. Only a minority of the Jews are worshipers of Jehovah, and very few know Jesus as Messiah. But when Russia is destroyed just before crushing Israel, many will call upon God and Israel will not desecrate God's name anymore. Evidently even the Zionist leaders of Israel, many of whom are atheists today, will turn to the God of their fathers. That they will also trust in Christ at this time is doubtful, for his personal revelation to them is still in the future.

Although it is dangerous to hypothesize in areas where the Scriptures are not specific, this passage makes us wonder if there will be a brief worldwide spirit of revival before the end of the age. It is true that apostasy will increase, and we shall study that. And moral conditions will get worse, and we shall study that also. But when the world receives the electrifying news of the mysterious destruction of Russia, might there not be a tremendous harvest of souls? The prophet informs us that the result of communism's destruction will be the nations' recognition that God is the Lord. This is repeated twice in the passage, and is used in conjunction with "sanctifying" and "magnifying" God in the eyes of the people. That which glorifies God most is the salvation and sanctification of souls. This could mean that millions may be won to Christ between the destruction of Russia and the rise of the Antichrist.

EZEKIEL 38–39 NOT ARMAGEDDON

Many prophecy students are inclined to make the destruction of Russia as described in Ezekiel synonymous with the Battle of Armageddon that conquers the Antichrist. In so doing they place an unnecessary burden of interpretation on this passage and ignore several lines of reasoning clearly indicating to me that the two mass movement of troops cannot be considered the same. I would like to suggest several major differences and reasons why Ezekiel 38–39 must take place before or at the very beginning of the seven-year tribulation period.

The so-called Battle of Armageddon, as described by the prophet John in Revelation 16:12-21, comes at the end of the Tribulation period. Even a casual reading of Ezekiel's prophecy indicates two confederacies of nations, which is not possible under the world dominion of the Antichrist during the Tribulation. Another thing to keep in mind is that all the "kings of the earth" will be gathered in the Armageddon conflict (Revelation 16:14), whereas in Ezekiel's prophecy only Russia and its cohorts are involved. Another difference is that the armies gathered at Armageddon are arrayed against Christ (Revelation 19:19), not Israel as in Ezekiel's prophecy. Still another difference is that Christ will judge the nations after Armageddon, whereas Israel and other nations call upon God in confession and praise after Russia's debacle.

A reasonable conclusion to all of this is that Ezekiel's prophecy does not describe the same conflict as that called by God "he Battle of Armageddon." Since Armageddon comes at the end of human history, the destruction of Russia will come earlier.

RUSSIA'S TIMETABLE

The time of Russia's destruction is not difficult to calculate when we add certain information to these conclusions. Very simply, it must take place before the Tribulation period!

The Tribulation period is Israel's great testing time known in Jeremiah 30:7 as "Jacob's trouble." Most prophecy students have identified this period as the final seven years in the 490-year prophecy concerning Israel and her final deliverance as found in Daniel 9:24-27. The conditions on the earth during that time are given in great detail in the book of Revelation, chapters 6 through 18, and are described by Jesus in Matthew 24, as we saw earlier. Because so many events are known about this period, we can easily compare them with the events of Ezekiel's prophecy. For the following reasons, our conclusion is that Russia will be destroyed by God before the Tribulation begins.

1. Israel is seen by Ezekiel as dwelling securely in her land when Russia tries to invade. But Revelation 12:13-17 indicates that the Antichrist will attack Israel, breaking his covenant made at the beginning of the Tribulation (Daniel 9:27) and will launch the greatest anti-Semitic crusade the world has ever seen, scattering Jews all over the world.

2. During the tribulation period, the world will be governed by Antichrist (Revelation 13:1-7). As we have seen, there are two confederations of nations plus Israel in the Ezekiel prophecy. Since Antichrist sets up his world kingdom at the beginning of the Tribulation, the attack by the northeastern confederation must take place *before* the Tribulation.

3. Israel spends seven years burning the Russian implements of war: "And they that dwell in the cities of Israel shall go forth, and shall set on fire and burn the weapons, both the shields and the bucklers, the bows and the arrows, and the handstaves, and the spears, and they shall burn them with fire

seven years, so that they shall take no wood out of the field, neither cut down any out of the forests; for they shall burn the weapons with fire; and they shall spoil those that spoiled them, and rob those that robbed them, saith the Lord God" (Ezekiel 39:9-10).

These verses do not suggest that Israel couldn't burn the abandoned Soviet war materials in less than seven years, but instead of gathering firewood in winter they use these implements. Since it will take seven years to burn them, when will they do it? Certainly not the first seven years of the millennial kingdom, for after the Battle of Armageddon, which ushers in the millennial kingdom, swords will be beaten into plowshares (Isaiah 2:4), not burned! The only conclusion we can draw is that Russia will attack Israel before the Tribulation.

In this connection it is rather interesting to consider the report from Holland by John Weston. After he spoke on this subject, a Dutchman gave him a note reading, "I use a special wood for 'coke breakers'; this is stronger than steel springs and very elastic; the name is lignostone, invented by a Dutchman in Terapel; I am the superintendent of the Delft Gas Works." Weston was given some scraps of this wood and found that it burned better than coal. After returning to England he was told that this substance was now being used for cogs in the wheels of English lorries. He told all this to a friend later, who showed him an article reporting that the Russians were now using lignostone in the manufacturing of some of their weapons of war![15] This passage on the burning of war material has been difficult to explain because of the widespread use of steel in such items. It is more than passing strange that the very nation whose weapons will be destroyed by burning is the first on record to innovate wood in such manufacturing. Could it be a coincidence? If lignostone burns "better than coal" it would explain why Israel burns it for seven winters.

PRE-MID-POST TRIBULATIONISTS

Prophecy students are certain to ask at this point: "If Russia attacks Israel before the Tribulation period, does this mean it will occur before Christ raptures the Church?" Before we answer that question, we should remind the reader what is meant by the "Rapture of the Church." The word *rapture* is used to describe a Greek term expressing the sudden disappearance from this earth of all true believers in Christ. The word literally means to "snatch away," and indicates that one day Christ will shout from heaven, dead believers will be resurrected, living believers will be "changed" (as Christ's body was after his resurrection), and all will gather in the clouds "to meet the Lord in the air." This event is detailed in 1 Thessalonians 4:13-18 and 1 Corinthians 15:51-58. Read both passages if you are not familiar with the event, and review chapter 2.

At the risk of sounding too theological, I should explain that three views of the Rapture or coming of Christ for his Church are held by prophecy students. All believe in the literal coming of Christ for his Church. However, some feel he will come in the middle of the Tribulation, some hold to his coming at the end of the Tribulation, and the majority believe the Bible teaches he will come before the Tribulation. All three have their reasons for believing as they do, and I have found some very dedicated Christians in each group.

To this writer it seems quite certain that Christ will come for his Church before the Tribulation, and some of the reasons for saying so are as follows:

1. The second coming is called "the blessed hope" in Titus 2:13. Anyone who understands the awful days of the Tribulation as described in Revelation 6–18 can appreciate why Christ's deliverance of his people from these horrors is called the "blessed hope"!

2. First Thessalonians 1:10 and Revelation 3:10 clearly

indicate that the Church is to be "delivered from the wrath to come," or, "I also will kee   thee from the hour of temptation, which shall come upon all the world to try them that dwell upon the earth." The Tribulation period, the time of Jehovah's "wrath," will try the whole earth. The Church, then, is promised deliverance from that judgment.

3. Second Thessalonians 2:1-8 provides the chronological basis for the pretribulation position. The subject is the Second Coming of Christ (verse 1), with specific reference to two events in it: "our gathering together unto him" and "the day of the Lord." "The day of the Lord" is the time of God's judgment upon the wicked nations of the earth. Our "gathering together unto him" is quite a different event. Before "the day of the Lord" arrives, Paul says "the man of sin" (Antichrist) must be revealed. The chart above will clarify this teaching.

4. The Tribulation is a period of judgment on the earth compared in Scripture to God's judgments in the days of Noah and the days of Lot. Since God delivered Noah and his family before the flood, and since he delivered Lot and his daughters before the destruction of Sodom, it seems quite reasonable that he will follow this procedure and deliver the Church before the Tribulation judgments.

All of this has a bearing on whether Christians may see the destruction of Russia before the Rapture. If the Church will be raptured in the middle or at the end of the Tribulation, of course we will see the invasion of Israel by Russia; but if Christ does indeed come for his Church prior to the Tribulation, there is a strong possibility we will not see it.

A PRETRIBULATION MISCONCEPTION

A very common misconception of those who hold to the pretribulation Rapture position is that the Rapture of the Church

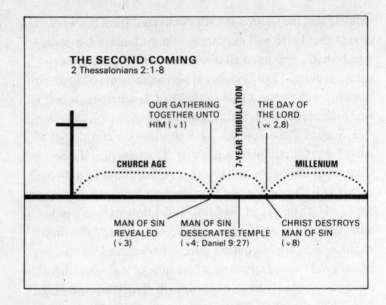

begins the Tribulation. According to Daniel 9:27, the signing of a political covenant between Israel and the Antichrist for seven years inaugurates the Tribulation. Some have assumed that the events are simultaneous, but there is nothing in the Scripture to indicate this. Because the Rapture at the end of the Church age coincides *approximately* with the beginning of the Tribulation period, many have made that assumption.

Nothing in prophecy forbids the possibility of an interim period between these events. Suggestions of prophecy teachers have run anywhere from a week to twenty-five years. Those who favored the long periods wrote many years ago when it seemed there were a number of events still awaiting fulfillment. If they lived today I am confident they would shorten their estimates.

With all this background, we may now proceed with the question: Will Russia invade Israel before the Rapture? A very simple answer would be: It's possible, but I wouldn't count on it. I say this because it seems there is a possibility that a brief, worldwide reorganizational period will follow the destruction of Russia, during which time many people will turn to Christ, and then he will come to Rapture his Church. However, it is also possible that Christ will first come for his Church, Russia will invade Israel, and then the Antichrist will make his covenant with Israel. The Bible simply is not definite on this point. The only passages of which I am aware that touch on this are the deliverances from judgment already mentioned — Lot and Noah. Here we find that the day Noah entered into the ark the floods came, and the day Lot went out of Sodom it rained fire and brimstone (Luke 17:27-30).

The time between the Rapture and Israel's signing of the covenant with the Antichrist could be a day or a short period. If a period of time separates them, we will not see Russia's destruction; if it's just one day, Russia's defeat would seem to precede the Rapture. Since the Scripture is not clear on the subject, it is dangerous to be dogmatic on the issue. The best thing for Christians is to be prepared either way. As our Lord said many times, "Watch and be ready, for in such an hour as you think not, the Son of man cometh." Make sure you are ready whether he comes before or after the invasion of Russia. If, however, you see the destruction of Russia as she attempts to invade Israel, you can expect the Rapture of the Church very soon.

If the magnifying and sanctifying of the Lord, as indicated in Ezekiel 38:16, 23, and 39:7, 13, 22, does indeed mean a short period of time when men call upon the Lord as a result of his mir-aculous preservation of Israel, then we should work diligently to prepare for it. Since we can expect the period to be brief, we should begin now to train ourselves and find positions of service where we can reach a maximum number of people with the gospel.

Actually, the best harvesters during that soul-harvest period will be those who are reaching a maximum number of people for Christ today. Every Christian should consider ways of expanding his ministry today so he will be ready to step into a key position of influence in that day.

No one knows how long we have before we see the fulfillment of these things, but as we shall see in future studies, it seems that it cannot be much longer before our Lord comes for his Church. As the Lord Jesus said, although we cannot predict the "day or the hour" (Matthew 24:36) when he shall return, we can know the season. This book is dedicated to showing that we are not only in the season, but the twilight of the season.

1. Hal Lindsey, *The Late Great Planet Earth* (Grand Rapids: Zondervan, 1970) pp. 64-65.
2. Walter Chamberlain, *The National Resources and Conversion of Israel* (London, 1854).
3. Louis Bauman, *Russian Events in the Light of Bible Prophecy* (Philadelphia: The Balkiston Co., 1952).
4. John Cumming, M.D., *The Destiny of Nations* (London: Hurst & Blackette, 1864).
5. Wilhelm Gesenius, D.D., *Hebrew and English Lexicon* (Grand Rapids: Eerdmans, 1949).
6. C. F. Keil, D.D. and F. Delitzsch, D.D., *Biblical Commentary on the Old Testament* (Grand Rapids: Eerdmans, 1949).
7. Gesenius, *op. cit.*
8. Cumming, *op. cit.*
9. Gesenius, *op. cit.*
10. Gesenius, *op. cit.*
11. W. S. McBirnie, *The Coming Decline and Fall of the Soviet Union* (Glendale, California: Center for American Research and Education).
12. Robert Young, LL.D. *Young's Analytical Concordance* (Grand Rapids: Eerdmans, 1955).
13. Gesenius, *op. cit.*
14. Lindsey, *op. cit.,* pp. 67-71.
15. "Russian War Implements, Fuel for Israel," by John Weston, The *Mt. Zion Reporter.*

SIX
CAPITAL AND
LABOR CONFLICTS

Progress, though desirable, often produces unforeseen conflicts. Bible prophecy does not have that limitation, for there the end is known from the beginning.

A little-known but valid sign of our Lord's return is found in James 5:1-5. The proper reading of this text makes clear that it concerns the last days. Unlike the previous signs, it would not stand alone as a clear indication of the lateness of earth's hour. However, when placed beside those we have studied and others that will follow, it provides one more indication that God's prophetic clock is moving steadily, bringing us into the last minutes of the end of the age.

"Go to now, ye rich men, weep and howl for your miseries that shall come upon you. Your riches are corrupted and your garments are moth-eaten. Your gold and silver is cankered; and the rust of them shall be a witness against you, and shall eat your flesh as it were fire. Ye have heaped treasure together for the last days. Behold, the hire of the laborers who have reaped down your fields, which is of you kept back by fraud, crieth; and the cries of them which have

reaped are entered into the ears of the Lord of Sabaoth. Ye
have lived in pleasure on the earth, and been wanton; ye
have nourished your hearts, as in a day of slaughter" (James
5:1-5).

Several characteristics of this prophecy are so common
today that they scarcely need specific verification. The first is
that riches will be accumulated by some, yet will not become
a source of happiness; instead, they will produce misery and
heartache. Frequently in the counseling room I have com-
mented on the complete inability of riches to bring happiness,
and in recent years I have interviewed a number of people
who possess an abundance of material goods, but they "weep
and howl" for the miseries that have come upon them.

In order to accumulate wealth the husband has to work
night and day, neglecting the wife of his youth. When their
income has risen, she hires a maid and then is bored because
there is not enough to do. Recently a Christian periodical carried the story of an automobile dealer who came home after
twenty-five years to tell his wife he had finally hit his goal —
he was worth a million dollars. But when he reached the
house he was served with divorce papers. His wife was tired
of being neglected for his business. Fortunately, this man was
led to Christ as a result of this trauma and God reestablished
his home on Jesus Christ, not his riches. He found that happiness "consisteth not in those things that a man possesseth."

How well I remember the tragic man who had made a quar-
ter of a million dollars in one year. He drove a new Lincoln
Continental, his clothes were the finest — he was miserable.
Halfway through our counseling session he sadly related,
"When we were first married, we were so poor that all we
could do was stay home and play Scrabble in front of the fire.
But I think we were far happier then than we are now, even
though we can afford to do anything we want." These are

not isolated cases. I could give many others from my own counseling ministry, and in talking with others I find there is a growing disenchantment with material possessions. They tend to produce misery rather than blessing.

You have no doubt heard of the "junk bond" scams that resulted in at least one famous stockbroker going to jail for eight years. That was followed by the "S & L bail out" by the federal government that will yet cost taxpayers over half a trillion dollars. Both situations were caused by greed and a "get rich quick" obsession.

One fact of this prophecy indicates that men will heap treasures to themselves in the last days. Although there have always been a few rich and many poor, monumental fortunes are being made today, and, as this text indicates, at the expense of the working man. In recent years we have witnessed the amalgamation of many companies, and because of the tremendous tax advantages we have observed the rise of "conglomerates."

The main characteristic of this prophecy involving conflict between capital and labor indicates the "cries" of the laborers have reached the Lord. A quick glance at history will show that we have experienced more worldwide conflicts between labor and management than ever before. Since the Russian revolution of 1917, when the needs of the laboring man were used as an excuse to form a social revolution, we have seen a tremendous increase of the labor movement being in conflict with management. As a boy I used to hear of occasional strikes. Today we speak of a round of strikes. Strikes by steel workers, automobile workers, police, school teachers, grape pickers, railroad workers, and recently I read of a planned "housewives' strike." We have no reason to think it will get any better! Inflationary prices follow wage increases, taxes take their toll, and then it's time for another round of strikes.

The interesting thing, however, is that the closer we get to the end of the age, the more pronounced and far-reaching do these conflicts between labor and capital become. And they are not limited to American free enterprise. We find the same reports coming from England, Germany, France, Italy, India, Japan, and anywhere else that man enjoys freedom. Of course, strikes do not occur in Communist countries, but they don't have freedom.

The final part of this prophecy of the last days that we shall consider is taken from James 5:5: "Ye have lived in pleasure on the earth, and been wanton; ye have nourished your hearts, as in a day of slaughter." This tragic indictment describes conditions that exist today. How well I remember that I was a sophomore in college when I first ate in a restaurant. Today one of the fastest growing businesses is the restaurant trade. Thirty years ago our city offered only a handful of good eating places; today there are so many good ones that it is difficult to make a selection. Evidently more people are living "in pleasure" than ever, for these places would not stay open unless they were patronized. In fact, most of them have a waiting list, and this tendency seems to be general in big cities the world over.

That men are living for pleasure today will occupy us in a later prophecy. Suffice it to say here that we are witnesses to the increase in the pleasure-seeking rich, many of whom attempt to gain profit at the expense of the poor. We also have observed conflict and stress among owners and workers, and people living "in pleasure." Our conclusion is obvious: this prophecy, being fulfilled in our own time to a greater degree than ever before, is additional evidence that God's prophetic clock is moving closer to the end time.

SEVEN
SKYROCKETING TRAVEL AND KNOWLEDGE

"But thou, O Daniel, shut up the words, and seal the book, even to the time of the end; many shall run to and fro, and knowledge shall be increased" (Daniel 12:4).

"Unbelievable" is the term most often used to describe the technology of our day. It compares only with fiction of a generation past, yet today it is reality. We have automatic gadgets, computers, and missiles that existed only in the creative minds of men like Jules Verne in the past century. And all this advancement is based on man's accumulated knowledge, just as the prophet Daniel predicted for the end time.

Daniel had doubtless never traveled faster than on horseback, and probably his most common speed was his walking pace. In fact, that was the speed of all men until about the middle of the 19th century. With the invention of steam engines and experimentation with electric power, man was sent flying down the roads and rivers at speeds of five to nineteen miles per hour. The genius of Henry Ford produced the internal combustion engine and the "horseless carriage." It wasn't long before speed limits of twenty-five, thirty-five, and now sixty-five miles per hour were posted. Today we have cars that travel at six hundred, planes that hurtle through the air at two thousand, and space ships at twenty-four thousand miles per hour.

These astronomical accelerations in speed have given rise to an unprecedented increase in travel, just as Daniel the prophet predicted for "the time of the end" when "many shall run to and fro." I could not help thinking about that prophecy one night as I looked out a plane window while preparing to land in Los Angeles. The freeways were crowded with cars "running to and fro." Today one of the greatest problems facing officials in our major cities is what to do with the fantastic traffic snarls. Freeways cannot be built fast enough to accommodate the desire of people to "run to and fro." This problem, of course, is not limited to America. I have been in London, Paris, Italy, Bombay, Calcutta, Japan, Manila, and many other places in the world, and I do not know one major city where this problem does not exist.

The desire to travel is certainly not limited to the ground. In the early 1960s the transportation department stated that more than 140 million passengers were transported by airlines. Since then we have seen the 707 and 727 almost double the speed of such commercial flights. The 747 has doubled the passenger carrying capability. The Concord, which travels faster than the speed of sound, commutes between Europe and other major capitals on a regular basis.

In our country we have witnessed the change from "an occasional trip to town" to frequent trips to all parts of the country. There was a day, not too long ago, when it was a novelty to meet a person who had traveled in Europe. Today we all know a dozen or more people who have been there. I was eighteen years old before I had left the state of Michigan. In fact, only rarely did I travel more than a hundred miles from Detroit. When my son was sixteen years old, he flew one weekend to Washington, D.C., participated in a victory march to the White House, toured the Naval Academy at Annapolis, and was home in time to attend school Monday morning. A six-thousand-mile trip, and he didn't miss a class! How many people dreamed fifty years ago that such a thing would be possible?

Recently I read that commercial airlines will someday have planes traveling at Mach 2 and Mach 3 speeds — twenty-five hundred to thirty-five hundred miles per hour. The writer said it will be possible for people to live in New York and work in Los Angeles; in fact, it may take longer to commute from the suburbs to La Guardia Field than to fly across the country.

A businessman in Racine, Wisconsin, told me that he met a Jewish man in Florida who had just moved his family to Israel. He was employed as a pilot on one of the major airlines and commuted to work in the United States. That could be done only in this age of high-speed travel.

Much more could be said to prove that we are traveling "to and fro" more than ever before, but the facts are so well known that they deserve little further consideration. Most interesting, however, is the historical moment when this tendency to travel really began. A quick look at history will show that back in 1913, when Henry Ford organized the first assembly line and mass produced one million Model T Fords, the riding speed was about twenty-five miles per hour. The next year the world was thrust into World War I, the great sign of the end, and this catapulted all nations into a race to transport men "to and fro."

World War I saw more men leave their homes and loved ones, fight on foreign soil, and return than was true in all the wars of history. It was World War I that saw the first use of underwater vessels to transport men to and fro. It was World War I that saw the first use of airplanes as instruments of destruction and combat. Once again we are confronted with the fact that the monumental event regarding the end of the age was the great sign of 1914–1918.

Several years ago the telephone company put out a booklet about the speed of travel. I have wished many times I had saved it because it contained a graph showing the rate at which speeds have increased. The line of speed paralleled the line of history for centuries. About the middle of the nineteenth century, it started up slightly; after World War I it made a sharp incline; and today the chart line is going almost straight up. The telephone company did not realize it was graphically illustrating the fulfillment of Bible prophecy.

Man's ability to "run to and fro" has been made possible by his tremendous increase in knowledge. It has been estimated that from the days of the flood until the year 1800, man's total knowledge only doubled once. "In the next hundred years, man's knowledge doubled again. We are told by scientists that man's knowledge is doubling about every ten to fifteen years."[1]

It has been estimated that 70 percent of the medicines in use today were developed after World War II. More than 80 percent of the scientists who have ever lived are alive today! And high-speed computers can classify and sort information today in unbelievable time. An engineer friend told me he can press a few buttons on a computer and in thirty minutes duplicate an engineer's life work produced before 1955.

The quest for knowledge goes on at an ever-heightening pace. College enrollments are exploding all over the world. In our own country the number of college students has doubled in the last decade. Today 46 percent of America's youth between the ages of eighteen and twenty-one are attending some kind of post-high school institution.

We hear a great deal about revolution today, little noticing that a revolution in knowledge is going on all around us. Have you looked at your children's textbooks lately? My seventh-grade daughter asked me to help her with math homework once, and she ended up giving me an education in "new math." A group of psychiatrists in Los Angeles a few months ago had a conference to consider the knowledge explosion and its effect on the family. Their solution was typically humanistic. Due to the fact that parents were not keeping up with the increase in knowledge and in order to keep from retarding the rate of their children's learning, the government should make plans to raise our children in the future, they said!

During the last twenty years the computer has revolution-ized many forms of research and learning. Today it is able to do the work formerly done by thousands of workers. The Sperry Rand Corporation has developed a memory bank which can assimilate the 850,000 words in the Bible five times in one second!

A well-known Christian counselor is dreaming of feeding every conceivable emotional, family, and personal problem known to man into a memory bank. A team of Bible experts will then provide an excellent Bible answer to each problem. Counseling computer centers can be placed all over the coun-try, where laymen can give written tests or questionnaires to counselees. The information would then be fed into the com-puter, and the very best possible Bible answer would be placed in the individual's hand in a matter of minutes.

The Wycliffe Bible Translators wasted no time using the computer to speed up their work of translating the Bible into every language of the world. One of the missionaries our church supports, Joe Grimes, is one of the world's leading authorities on linguistics. Having already translated the entire

New Testament into the Huichol Indian language, he pioneered the use of computers in translation at the University of Mexico. According to Dr. Grimes, they have so speeded up the process that it is now possible for a missionary to do a complete translation in ten years, whereas formerly it took thirty. That means it is now conceivable for a missionary to translate the Word of God into three languages instead of just one during his lifetime, and Wycliffe is working continuously to cut the time even more.

Why is all of this so important? Not only has this explosion in knowledge made possible the running of man "to and fro" on the earth, but it is a fulfillment of Daniel's prophecy that "at the time of the end . . . knowledge shall be increased." A recent translation of that verse is even more suggestive: "There will be a sudden knowledge explosion." We submit to the reader that the accurate fulfillment of this sign, accelerating as it is with each passing decade, particularly since World War I, is another "birth pain" and movement of the hands on God's prophetic clock, bringing us close to the end of this age.

Unfortunately for mankind, this vast acquisition of knowledge does not seem to bring him any closer to obtaining wisdom than he was before. In fact, it seems to me that many educators of our day are further from wisdom than ever. My counseling ministry has convinced me that just having a Ph.D. degree doesn't necessarily produce better interpersonal relationships. Some of the most emotionally maladjusted people I have dealt with have been those with the greatest education.

Another frightening thing about this accumulation of knowledge is that it has made man more self-sufficient and independent from God. I have found it far more difficult to get a Ph.D. to humble himself before God than a high school graduate — and not because he faces too many intellectual obstacles (there aren't that many that discredit faith), but his problem is one of ego. His accumulation of knowledge tends to make him too proud to bend his knees to Jesus Christ. In short, he demonstrates that it is possible to have knowledge without wisdom.

What is wisdom? The Bible says many times, "The fear of the Lord is the beginning of wisdom." That is, the reverential awe or respect for the Lord is the beginning of wisdom. Until a man has worshiped God through Jesus Christ his Son, he has not learned wisdom. It is possible to have both knowledge and wisdom. I have met a number of humble and brilliant scholars throughout the world who are wise toward God. If you have neglected true wisdom for knowledge, may I suggest that you pursue that as vigorously as you have knowledge. Start out by receiving Jesus Christ as your Lord and Savior by simple faith. Study the Word of God to show yourself "approved unto God, a workman that needeth not to be ashamed, rightly dividing the word of truth" (2 Timothy 2:15). The result will be the wisdom of God.

1. F. Kenton Beshore, *What Are the Signs of the Last Days?* (Los Angeles: Biblical Research Society, 1965), p. 82.

EIGHT
APOSTASY

A very discouraged and disillusioned young reporter from the *San Diego Union* came into my office. As religion editor, he was interviewing local ministers to get their views on the resurrection of Jesus Christ for a pre-Easter series of articles. While we talked, a new hope came into his voice as he exclaimed, "You sure believe differently than the last three ministers I talked to!"

It seems he had discussed this matter with three liberal pastors representing different denominations in our city. To his amazement and obvious disappointment, none of them believed in the bodily resurrection of Jesus Christ. The strange thing about it was that the editor did not claim to be a Christian. He was really shaken, however, by the unbelief of those clergymen because, as he said, "If ministers don't believe in the resurrection, what hope is there for the rest of us?"

After hearing the gospel simply presented, this man prayed to receive Christ. I guess the theological shock was good for him. A few weeks later I invited him to a gathering of evangelical ministers where Henry M. Morris, former head of the

Civil Engineering Department at Virginia Polytechnic Institute and now academic head of our new Christian Heritage College, was to speak on "Miracles and Natural Science." There it was my privilege to introduce this much-relieved reporter to Dr. Morris and sixty-five ministers who heartily believe in the bodily resurrection of Jesus Christ.

Unfortunately, many of the victims of this liberal religious heresy are not confronted with the truth and stumble around in spiritual ignorance. We should not be surprised by such a tragic drift from "the faith which was once delivered unto the saints" (Jude 2-3) since it is clearly presented to us in the New Testament. The Bible predicted that such apostasy would be a sign of the end of the age. Consider the warning of the apostle Paul.

"Let no man deceive you by any means; for that day shall not come, except there come a falling away first, and that man of sin be revealed, the son of perdition" (2 Thessalonians 2:3).

Studied in context, the apostle is saying that before the day of the Lord and the revelation of the Man of Sin (in the Tribulation period), there will be a "falling away" first. The Greek word translated "falling away" is *apostasia*. It is the source word for "apostasy" and means to defect from the truth or depart from that which was given at the first. The plain meaning of this prophecy is that before Christ comes, many who once were entrusted with the truth would depart from it.

Anyone familiar with recent church history knows that this present generation has experienced more apostasy than any other—and it has its deepest roots in the days right after World War I. I know it was in existence before World War I, but since that time it has taken giant steps forward until today apostate religious leaders seem to outnumber the faithful ones. At least, they get more publicity.

There was a time when the average Christian could move to

a new city, attend the church of his denomination, and confi-
dently expect the same faithful message he was used to. That
day is long gone! Ever since 1918 it has become increasingly
difficult, and today I do not know of any major denomination
that does not have to admit with shame that some apostate
preachers fill their church pulpits, cloaked in their traditional
church names. The discerning church member now looks for
the content of a church's message more than the denominational tag. If he doesn't, he may find himself spiritually starv-
ing in a well-organized religious machine rather than growing
at a spiritual feeding station.

HOW DID IT HAPPEN?

Volumes have been written on the spread of apostasy, so
obviously we need not offer a detailed study here. But a few
points will be mentioned to show how powerful this movement has become, particularly in recent times. Of one thing I
am certain — the same devilish power that produced French
skepticism, German rationalism, Nietzscheism, communism,
socialism, and many other intellectual evils produced religious apostasy.

In the middle of the nineteenth century almost all denominations had one branch in the United States, and all of these
were basically fundamental — that is, they adhered to the
orthodox doctrines of the founders of their group. The Civil
War caused several of these denominations to split along
geographical lines, but the issues were social, not theological. Little was changed by the turn of the century. The
Church was still basking in the afterglow of the Charles A.
Finney evangelistic crusades, followed by those of D. L.
Moody and others. Certain individuals educated in Europe
and influenced by German rationalism began teaching in

denominational seminaries. The devil knew that the best way to inject his apostate doctrine into the churches was to infiltrate the seminaries, indoctrinate the young ministers, and send them into churches across the land to spread his false concepts. The faithfulness of these denominations to the Word of God today is in direct proportion to the success of denominational leaders in keeping heretics out of their seminaries two generations ago. It is a constant fight! Some that won the battle during the first half of this century seem to be losing it now.

One illustration of the effectiveness of this devilish method is a now-deceased seminary professor. For more than twenty-five years he occupied "the chair of Christian ethics" in what was the largest seminary in the nation. He helped to orient the thinking of thousands of present-generation ministers. Several years ago this man was identified under oath as a member of the Communist party by four undercover agents of the F.B.I. before reputable investigative bodies of our government. Is it any wonder that his denomination is the most radical and unbelieving in Christendom? I hope you see that it wouldn't take many such men, working consistently through the years, to turn an entire denomination away from the faith of the Bible.

This man's forerunners must have been at work prior to and during World War I, because modernism became increasingly powerful shortly after 1920 and openly challenged funda-mentalists for control of the seminaries and, quite frequently, of the denominations. Sad to say, in many cases they won.

Since those days fragmentation has been the organizational result. Many churches and groups broke with their parent denomination and started their own; later some of these splin-tered off again. Today there are hundreds of Protestant groups and denominations. For example, the group in which I am a member had only one denomination in this country one hundred and twenty years ago. At last count there were twenty-nine. Although this fragmentation is a threat to organization-minded ecumenists, we shall see in a later study that it does tend to make the individual churches dependent more directly on the Holy Spirit and less on denominational machinery.

In some big denominations, local congregations have had little to say about the calling of a minister and power has been centralized in the hands of a few. Under these conditions, aggressive apostates have gained much influence. Millions of members have faced the decision whether to stay in the denomination or pull out and start a new church. Those who have "stayed with the ship" have seemingly not stopped the consistent drift toward apostasy.

Liberal churchmen organized the Federal Council of Churches in the 1940s, but it became so ultraliberal and pro-Communist that laymen abandoned it in large numbers. It was dissolved and the National Council of Churches of Christ in America became the spokesman for cultural Christianity. Although the structure was changed slightly, a close look at the people in charge revealed a game of musical chairs; many of the former leaders directed the new Council. This religious organization has accelerated the churches' departure from the Bible and sent it deeper into apostasy. But it seems to be foundering from its organizational weight, and many laymen have repudiated its social and political stands. Through neglecting and rejecting Bible teachings, this organization has been instrumental in bringing in practices and programs that border on blasphemy.

The modernism of the first part of the century was too radical for many people and even some leaders, so a new group of theologians introduced neo-orthodoxy in the thirties, wherein they used some of the same language as the fundamentalists but meant something different. This subterfuge has deceived many. Some in this apostate movement degenerated to the point that a number of seminary professors launched the "God is dead" movement. They claim to be "Christian atheists," whatever that is supposed to mean.

Relationships between socialistic politics and theological apostasy have been consistent. The early modernists rejected the basic teachings of Christianity such as the virgin birth of Christ, his deity, his physical resurrection, his Second Coming, man's innate sinfulness, and many other essential doctrines. Since that left them no spiritual message for the people, they came up with the social gospel. This has been the one consistent chord of the apostate movement in America and has thrust them into the forefront of the social revolution.

Apostate ministers have shocked the sensibilities of their congregations beyond imagination with their blasphemous statements and equally outlandish innovations. We have seen some of them become leading exponents of the "sexual revolution," creating what they call the "new morality," which in common practice often turns out to be no morality. One major denomination which originally was known for its adherence to the Word of God has successfully changed its four-hundred-year-old confession of faith to conform to more "progressive" beliefs. They faced strong opposition on the floor of their convention because their denomination still contains leaders who believe the Word of God. But their subtlety and growing influence overcame the opposition and superseded the old, sound creed with a modernized, something-for-everyone confession.

More recently this denomination was shaken by a "progressive" report from its thirty-three-member council on church and society. Its unscriptural view of sex stirred great controversy in that religious body before being officially accepted.

The denomination hastened to assure its people that the report
was not approved but merely accepted. This report is worthy
of our consideration because it was not designed by laymen
but by ministers and seminary professors. The chairman of the
committee is professor of pastoral theology at "one of the
denominations' leading divinity schools." The report was so
sensational that it was written up by both *Parade* and *Look*
magazines and, needless to say, it stirred no little controversy
in the three-million-member denomination. Because it repre-
sents apostate thinking, I am quoting from the *Look* article.

"To increasingly large numbers of young people . . . being a
virgin at marriage proves nothing by itself. More significant is
one's personal maturity and readiness to accept joyously the
responsibilities of life together. To put it plainly, fewer and
fewer young people are willing to think of a non-virgin as a
'fallen' person. . . . A courtship which has helped a couple
develop profound sensitivities to each other and tenderness in
response to each other's needs and desires can prepare them
for a healthy adjustment of their sexual energies in the marriage that follows. If in the course of such a courtship, a
couple has taken a responsible decision to engage in premari-
tal intercourse, the church should not convey to them the
impression that their decision is in conflict with their status as
members of the body of Christ.

"In sexual relations between married couples, the committee believes nothing ought to be 'forbidden except that which
offends the sensibilities of one's partner.'"[1]

This report goes on to encourage the church to free people
from feelings of guilt at practicing masturbation. It further suggests that the church be more understanding with homosexuals
and disagrees with the apostle Paul's teachings on this subject.

Currently several mainline churches have ordained
women into the pastoral ministry, contrary to both Christian

church tradition and the writing of Scripture. And recently an Episcopal bishop who ordained an acknowledged homosexual priest is calling for his church to perform homosexual marriages. Such heretical innovations are even pursued in the face of the widespread killer disease AIDS — a primarily sexually transmitted disease.

Any Bible student can see what a far cry this is from the true teaching of the Scriptures. With men who think like this training future generations of ministers, it is not surprising that many young clerics today in the apostate movement spend more time demonstrating or serving time in jail for demonstrating illegally on issues of civil rights than they do in leading people to Christ.

Nor is it surprising to find that in an attempt to be "progressive," some churches have conducted folk or rock communion and worship services. One church in Boston described in *Newsweek* opened its doors to eleven hundred teenagers and permitted them to conduct a rock and roll festival in the church. "A procession of boys and girls placed a Bible, bread and Coke, pool cue, and billiard ball on the communion table to symbolize religion, eating, and playing. Then a dozen teenagers, some in shorts, crowded into the church aisles to frug on the rug and do the watusi."[2]

Many more illustrations of the alarming growth of apostasy could be given, but the reader is probably already familiar with the fearful extent of the problem. The examples cited were selected to show existing trends and to prove that the "falling away" has already begun. According to prophecy it will continue until well after the Lord's return. Its rapid development, particularly in the past decade, should be a graphic warning to us that the end is close at hand.

If you happen to be one of those individuals who has been deceived by an apostate church, I have a suggestion other than turning aside from Christianity in disgust. Turn directly to Christ himself. He has not changed! His promises are just as valid today as when he gave them. If you have any questions as to whether or not you have called upon the name of the Lord personally to be saved, call upon him immediately. He is waiting for your call and promises instant response, for he has proclaimed: "Let him that is athirst come. And whosoever will, let him take of the water of life freely" (Revelation 22:17).

After receiving Christ, you should seek out a Bible-teaching church known for its faithfulness to the Scriptures.

1. *Look*, September 11, 1970.
2. *Newsweek*, May 9, 1966.

NINE
OCCULT SHADOWS—
AND REALITIES

"Now the Spirit speaketh expressly that, in the latter times, some shall depart from the faith, giving heed to seducing spirits, and doctrines of devils, speaking lies in hypocrisy, having their conscience seared with a hot iron" (1 Timothy 4:1-2).

The future has always had a strange fascination for man. It has taken many forms through the ages—fortunetellers, witches, soothsayers, palm and tea leaf readers, occultists, sorcerers. Today, just as the Bible prophesied, we are having an epidemic of such "seducing spirits and doctrines of devils."

Originally astrology and horoscope reading was done by Babylonian priests for the kings. Then the Greeks and Romans adopted the practice, and during the superstitious Middle Ages it swept through Europe. Luther called it a "shabby art," but many universities of his day had professional chairs of astrology. It faded during the rise of rationalism, but since the turn of this century there has been a consistent increase in its devotees. It experienced surges of interest after both world wars.

The Spiritualist Church in America was founded in 1906.[1] Since that time astrology has grown into a household word. Leading magazines dignify this fraud by showing beautiful color pictures of the signs of the zodiac and informing readers of the assumed implications of the names.

Horoscope reading is so widespread in this country today that most daily newspapers have a horoscope column. Thousands of people would not start their day without consulting their horoscope to find out whether it is going to be a good or bad day. The pure fraud of this thing has been ably exposed by the German scholar Kurt Koch.[2] He points out that one newspaper, due to the absence of fresh material, conceived the idea of running back issues of the column. They did this, and although they had over 100,000 readers, they did not receive one complaint until the twenty-second daily fraud was printed. The gullible are willingly deceived and the cult is growing.

A *Los Angeles Times* writer asserted that voodoo, black magic, and witchcraft are spreading all over the Southwest and probably the entire United States. In an interview with a modern-day witch, who otherwise was a typical American housewife, he learned that witchcraft is growing rapidly despite a fear of persecution. According to this young mother, whose husband is a supervisor in an aerospace firm, "Witchcraft has sprung to life with renewed vitality and thousands of new followers."[3]

The news media gave widespread publicity to a satanic wedding ceremony in San Francisco in February 1967. "An unemployed journalist married a former New York society figure with a nude woman as an altar."[4] The man who calls himself the "first priest of the Satanic Church" explained that the nude "symbolized the temple of the flesh, the epitome of earthly passion, earthly indulgence." He further indicated that newspaper publicity of his use of a nude had greatly helped his membership drive. You can be sure of one thing — the closer we get to the end of the age, the more we will observe the increase of Satan worship.

Occult manifestations of the spirit world are no longer scoffed at by our society. There are mediums, mystics, and prophetesses who have the ear of fashionable Washington society, and some have had close contact with the White House. One famous prophetess was the subject of a best-selling book after her unheeded prophecy about the death of former President Kennedy. Although not all of her visions have been accurate, she does have an uncanny number of predictions on target. One of her sensational visions, which has several unscriptural aspects and whose main character is a serpent, like the villain in the Garden of Eden, predicted that the Antichrist is living today, born in the 1960s.

This kind of spiritualist communication will increase for two reasons. Man is increasingly apprehensive about the future, and the Bible predicts an increase in satanic activity as we approach the end of the age. Witches, mediums, and false prophets were stoned to death by God-honoring Jews in Old Testament days (Deuteronomy 17:2-5). We don't recommend that procedure today, for it is contrary to civil law, but no Christians should get mixed up with this kind of thing! Instead, a Christian should know his Bible and so walk in the Spirit that he does not desire secret knowledge of the future. As has often been said, "We don't need to know the future if we are led by the one who holds the future."

Isaiah the prophet said, "Thou art wearied in the multitude of thy counsels. Let now the astrologers the stargazers, the monthly prognosticators, stand up, and save thee from these things that shall come upon thee. Behold, they shall be like stubble; the fire shall burn them; they shall not deliver themselves from the power of the flame; there shall not be a coal to warm at, nor fire to sit before it" (Isaiah 47:13-14).

Ultimately all witches, mediums, and those who permit their bodies to be used by Satan and his evil spirits to deceive men will be punished. But unfortunately they will deceive many before that day. The confused "age of Aquarius" is being deceived by these people, many of whom teach on the faculties of tax-supported colleges.

In the name of "academic freedom," the New Age movement has become common in our public schools. Parents across the country are voicing complaints that witchcraft, channeling, visualization techniques, and other hallmarks of the occult or outright Satanism are being practiced in our classrooms. In their attempt to indoctrinate the young, humanistic educators, protected by ACLU lawyers, have not considered the fact that these religious practices should be just as unwelcome as those they have excluded: Christianity, traditional moral values, and in some cases even the facts about our nation's religious history. Religious teaching, as long as it is not Christian, is welcome. Consequently, under the title "New Age," teaching any other religion is acceptable, from Satanism to Hinduism.

A young man in our church gave me a brochure from San Diego State College advertising a course in witchcraft. The course proved to be so popular that additional classes had to be scheduled. Our city does not have a monopoly on this bizarre academic excursion, for such studies are appearing on college curricula throughout the nation.

A housewife called to ask my advice about taking such a course. She acknowledged that she had been practicing mental telepathy and could tell what a person was going to say before he said it. I pointed out that she was cultivating a tendency that was forbidden by God for Christians. Reluctantly she gave up the practice, but today her spiritual life has overflowed to her family members, making that decision of obedience to her Lord one of the best she ever made.

SUPERNATURAL SIGNS

Several prophecies indicate that Satan and the Antichrist will use supernatural powers in the last days to deceive the people. Consider the following:

"Then shall that Wicked be revealed . . . even him whose coming is after the working of Satan with all power and signs and lying wonders, and with all deceivableness of unrighteousness in them that perish, because they received not the love of the truth, that they might be saved" (2 Thessalonians 2:8-10).

"And he doeth great wonders, so that he maketh fire come down from heaven on the earth in the sight of men, and deceiveth them that dwell on the earth by the means of those miracles which he had power to do in the sight of the beast, saying to them that dwell on the earth, that they should make an image to the beast, which had the wound by a sword, and did live. And he had power to give life unto the image of the beast, that the image of the beast should both speak, and cause that as many as would not worship the image of the beast should be killed" (Revelation 13:13-15).

Although these miraculous powers are scheduled for the Tribulation period, I would not be surprised if they begin to come to pass before then. Many of the other signs that culminate mainly in the Tribulation are already in motion today; because they take time, they have already been initiated. Such may very well be the case with signs and lying wonders. After all, the time of the greatest recorded demon activity in history was just prior to and during the first coming of Christ to the earth. Does it not follow that Satan, the master deceiver of men, will increase his activities again just before the Second Coming of Christ? It certainly seems that these evil powers have invaded many areas of life during the past few years.

TEST OF A PROPHET

As we foresee an increase in demon communication and miraculous signs, we should be very careful to know our Bible lest we be deceived along with millions of others. It is my personal feeling, though I do not wish to be dogmatic about it, that the texts above and others imply that Satan may attempt to duplicate the miracles of Jesus. One of the features of our Lord's miracles that repeatedly bring us face to face with his deity is that in almost two thousand years man has never duplicated his miracles. No one else has healed lepers with a spoken word, or created vision in sightless eyes by making a clay eyeball out of dirt, or fed a multitude of five thousand with one boy's lunch, having more left over than when he started. But since the Antichrist will be the antithesis of Jesus Christ, it seems likely he will try.

Since these activities *may* begin prior to the coming of our Lord, we had better learn to "try the spirits" to see if they are of God "because many false prophets are gone out into the world" (1 John 4:1). The following rules will serve as a simple guide to test every supernatural activity.

1. *Does the spirit (or person representing the spirit) confess "that Jesus Christ is come in the flesh"?* (1 John 4:2). Don't be deceived if spiritists are nice, gracious, pious sounding; they wouldn't deceive anyone if they were coarse, crude, and profane. It is not what they say that is important, but what they declare about Jesus the Christ that determines what they are. In this connection, don't be deceived by semantics; know

your Bible and really "try them." For it is possible to use clever words and say one thing while meaning quite another. For example, I know one heretic who tells Christian audiences he believes in the virgin birth of Christ. But in one of his books he points out that all people are virgin born when they are born in the love of God. Obviously he does not believe in the *physical* virgin birth. Others say they believe in the resurrection of Jesus, but they merely believe that the "spirit of Jesus" rose again and is in the world today. That is no bodily resurrection! But naive Christians fall for that line. Some false leaders say they believe the Bible is inspired, but they do not explain that they mean it is inspired like the writing of Shakespeare or Milton. In these last days we must carefully test the spirits concerning their acceptance of Jesus Christ as the eternal God.

2. *Does the message, prophecy, sign, or miracle glorify Jesus?* (John 16:13-14). The Christian is less likely to be deceived if he understands one thing at the outset: there are two sources of supernatural power — divine and demonic. The existence of a miracle does not guarantee its origin from God. There are many illustrations in the Bible where Satan had power to perform supernatural feats. You should also understand that Satan is a deceiver and a liar, so just seeing is not necessarily believing if he is involved. Fortunately for us, however, God is consistent. Everything he does is honest and according to principle. Therefore anything he does will glorify Jesus Christ. That is the express work of the Holy Spirit in these days and therefore a valid test for any teaching, prophecy, or miracle that confronts you.

3. *Does the person performing the sign or giving the prophecy teach anything that violates the clear teachings of the Word of God?* (Deuteronomy 13:1-5). This passage tells us that God sometimes tests us by permitting a false prophet to

have power and do things we cannot understand, to see if we love the Lord with all our hearts. At a time like that we must say, I won't believe what I see with my own eyes; I am going to believe the Word of God. In order to do that with safety, however, we must know God's Word, and that takes time. If ever there was a day when God's people should read, study, and memorize Scripture, it is today!

These simple tests can be applied by any Christian who wants to avoid being carried away with false teaching and errors. Paul predicted there would come a time when people would not "endure sound doctrine, but after their own lusts shall they heap to themselves teachers, having itching ears" (2 Timothy 4:3). Often Satan tries to get people to fall for his new schemes and plans by tempting them to lust. His new ideas and teachings usually contain a lowering of moral standards and a license to sin. This tendency is easy for the child of God to discern, as in the "new morality" of the apostate clerics of our day. Anyone who knows the Bible realizes that this is not a "new morality." It is the old immorality that has plagued man since Cain slew his brother Abel, since "the sons of God saw the daughters of men that they were fair, and they took them wives of all which they chose" — away back in the early chapters of Genesis (Genesis 6:2).

Be sure of this: God's standards never change! And we have no release from those standards just because we are living at the beginning of the end. It is time for God's people to heed his command in relation to the sins of lust, vice, spiritism, and witchcraft that surround them and avoid "the very appearance of evil."

Much of the interest in witchcraft and astrology today is caused by heart emptiness, so characteristic of those who do not know Jesus Christ. Some individuals are sincerely seeking direction through the layers of philosophical fog that surround them. Desperately seeking some source of supernatural guidance, they grasp at every new thing that comes along. If only they could hear and see that accepting Jesus Christ as their Savior and Lord would bring his Holy Spirit into their lives to guide them and to fill their emptiness! Because of faithful Christian witnesses, many are hearing and believing!

1. Norman B. Harrison, *His Sure Return* (Minneapolis: Harrison Service, 1952), p. 38.
2. Kurt Koch, *Between Christ and Satan* (Grand Rapids: Kregel, 1968), p. 17.
3. Bill Hazelett, "Witchcraft Bubbles, Boils; Old Black Magic Casting New Spell," *Los Angeles Times,* May 5, 1970.
4. Bob Distefano, *Pasadena Independent,* February 8, 1967.

TEN
PERILOUS TIMES

"This know, also, that in the last days perilous times shall come. For men shall be lovers of their own selves, covetous, boasters, proud, blasphemers, disobedient to parents, unthankful, unholy, without natural affection, trucebreakers, false accusers, incontinent, fierce, despisers of those that are good, traitors, heady, high-minded, lovers of pleasures more than lovers of God, having a form of godliness, but denying the power thereof; from such turn away" (2 Timothy 3:1-5).

Man's inhumanity to his fellow man is one of the most conspicuous elements of history, but ever since World War I it has reached gigantic proportions. At no time in world history has there been so much worldwide grief, affecting so many people, as has existed since 1914. More wars, revolutions, insurrections, and plagues have beset mankind than in any comparable period in history. More people are fearful, uptight, and filled with heartache than ever before, and that is exactly what the Bible predicted would happen in the last days (or the days just prior to the coming of Christ).

The "perilous times" of this passage has been translated

"grievous times" by some scholars. The Greek word actually means "outrageous" times. After examining the eighteen characteristics of the times as given here, you will find that they are outrageously evil times. Further, you will discover that every one of these characteristics is a common part of our national and international life, proving again that we are in the last days before the return of Christ. Consider these characteristics.

SELFISH MEN

"For men shall be lovers of their own selves." This certainly is a characteristic of our day. The "dog-eat-dog" concept of the pagan world was in marked contrast to the spirit of Christian compassion that prevailed in Western civilizations built on the gospel. But no longer! Even in America we sense a spirit of detachment and aloofness that prompts men and women to say, "I don't want to get involved." For instance, we were horrified by the story of the woman who was stabbed repeatedly on a dark New York street, and nearby residents who heard her cries not only refused to come to her aid but would not even call the police. Similar accounts appear in papers across the country, indicating that New Yorkers do not have a corner on callous selfishness.

This national spirit of self-love is not limited to relationships outside the home. As a counselor I have observed tragic signs of this sin creeping into the most significant relation-ship on earth—the family. Certainly the phenomenal rise in the divorce rate can be traced to the common problem of selfishness. In my book *How To Be Happy Though Married* I observed, "Everyone who has come to me with a marital problem has it because one or both of the partners is selfish." Twenty years have passed, and I have counseled thousands of others; I am still waiting to find the exception. Unselfish people do not develop marital problems they can't solve.

This increasing selfishness is also turning many children away from parents. God has given children a natural love for their parents, but I have seen selfish parents so reject and neglect their children that a wall of bitterness and hate has built up within the child, stifling his natural instincts. Within the last two weeks I have heard a selfish father describe his intense jealousy of his sons because of the attention shown by his wife to the boys, and an equally selfish wife confess her resentment of the affection showered by her husband on their little girls. Most marriages, particularly in homes where Christ is not known, go through such periods of difficulty or stress.

A generation ago parents would preserve the marriage for the children's sake and usually would find a way to resolve their differences. Today they are usually wrapped up so tightly in their own selfish desires they don't care about the children, or at least not as much about the children as they do themselves. "Don't I deserve some enjoyment out of life?" is the self-pitying cry I have heard many times from the selfish parent who "wants out." What they don't realize is that a change of partners doesn't change the cause of marital disharmony, which is selfishness.

This selfish spirit is not limited to the married, however. Recently a twenty-one-year-old young man announced, "If I ever get married I certainly won't have children. I hate kids!" His own childhood rejection and abandonment by his parents explains his selfish attitude, but it doesn't change it.

Have you ever wondered why this selfish spirit prevails today and where it comes from? The answer is very simple. When the philosophy of education in our country was based on Christian principles, children were taught responsibility to

God and others for their behavior—no man was a self-contained island. The false concept of evolution, which provided atheistic humanists with their main philosophical foundation, produces the erroneous conclusion that man is a high-level animal—and animals are naturally selfish! It is just that simple. Until man wakes up to the fact that he has been fed a gigantic lie in the name of education, he will degenerate as he blithely adopts more and more of the habits of animals.

COVETOUSNESS

Covetousness is the love of money or material possessions. This characteristic of the last days, with which the reader is familiar in our own country, is a result of selfishness. The crime wave we are experiencing today, led by robberies and thefts, also includes fraud, embezzlement, and deceit employed to amass material gains. What other reason than covetousness could motivate pornographers to print sexually inflammatory materials that stimulate crime and tragedy? What other motive causes dope peddlers to destroy the minds and lives of today's youth? Our selfish, materialistic philosophy has spawned a society of greedy monsters who frequently sell their souls for "a mess of pottage."

BOASTERS, PROUD

Pride, one of the sins God hates (Proverbs 16–17), is a hallmark of our day. The spirit of humility in leaders is rare anymore. Instead, we shamelessly brag about our children, possessions, and accomplishments. The spirit of keeping up with the Joneses is so strong that it is used by most advertising agencies in selling their products.

The sin of pride today is not limited to individuals, but

seems to be the attitude of governments and nations. Russia, China, Cuba, France, Israel, Egypt, and many other countries are examples. Saddam Hussein in Iraq is just a recent example.

Little emphasis seems to be placed on self-esteem or approval. Instead, the spirit of this age advocates that men seek the esteem of others. Evidently they have not realized the truth in Shakespeare's words, "To thine own Self be true." It is important to remember that loud-mouthed braggarts who pollute the air with their proud words are usually very insecure. They don't realize that humble honesty is mentally and emotionally healthful, whereas "pride leadeth to destruction."

BLASPHEMERS

The blasphemy of our society knows no bounds. In spite of the fact that the Word of God pointedly condemns those who take the name of God in vain (Exodus 20:7), profane blasphemy has become a part of everyday vocabulary. Prior to World War I it was never approved in mixed company or before children, even by the basest of men. There are even cases on record where men were challenged to duels for swearing in front of women. My high school football team was a profane group, but their profanity was reserved for the locker room. I remember two black players on our team beating up a black student in the hall one day for swearing in front of a girl. Interestingly enough, the girl was white.

Our nation's blasphemous tendencies are not limited to speech, however, but have invaded the fields of art, music, literature, education, and sad to say, religion. From nude portrayals of "love" on liberal church altars to desecration of altars dedicated to God, unbelievable blasphemy is being practiced today. Don't expect it to get any better as we approach the Antichrist climate of the last days.

One sidelight concerning blasphemy has often intrigued me. Profane men who use God's name in vain carelessly also use Jesus Christ's name the same way. In fact, I have debated atheists who repeatedly use Christ's name blasphemously. One such man said, "Jesus Christ was just a great philosopher." So I called his profane use of our Lord's name to his attention and pointed out that every time he did so, he was proving Jesus more than just a philosopher. Puzzled, he asked what I meant. I then queried, "If Jesus is just a philosopher, why don't you use other philosophers' names in vain? Have you ever heard a man curse in Aristotle's name, or Socrates' name? For that matter, have you ever heard men curse in Buddha's name or profanely use the names of Confucius and Mohammed?" I pointed out that when men want to curse, they are obliged to select the name of God — either God the Father or God the Son. This is easy for Christians to understand. Profanity and blasphemy are inspired by Satan, who doesn't care about blaspheming philosophers, or religious founders, but is especially intent on blaspheming God's name. This universal satanic tendency is a powerful evidence of the personal deity of Christ. It also suggests that we are in the last days, which will be the most anti-Christian days the world has ever known.

DISOBEDIENT TO PARENTS

In the early 1950s a writer delared, "Since World War I juvenile delinquency has exceeded anything ever known to civilization. Thousands of children in the roving bands of Europe and other thousands in America have left home or live in defiance of home authority. Modern life, geared to interests and attractions outside the home, facilitates this."[1]

The ensuing two decades have witnessed a juvenile delinquency problem of staggering magnitude. The flames

of resentment that seem most volatile in youthful hearts
have been exploited in the social revolution until young
people by the thousands are leaving home, school, and work
to "drop out."

Parents are repeatedly heard to exclaim, "I just can't do
a thing with that child!" The permissive philosophy of the
atheistic humanists has produced the most lawless generation of young people in all of history. Their rebellious activities are given front-page billing as they defiantly burn down
banks, colleges, and anything else that is an object of their
wrath.

What makes this generation so disobedient? Very simply,
failure of parents to teach their children to obey in the home.
Most of today's lawless youth were well on their way to rebellious conduct by the time they were five years old. The five-
year-old child who stamps his foot and screams to get his own
way, if indulged by his parents, will be fighting the police and
society ten years later. The Bible says, "He that spareth his
rod hateth his son; but he that loveth him chasteneth him
early" (Proverbs 13:24). God's Word is still the best manual
on human behavior, and unless we get back to living by its
principles, instead of the animal-like principles of man, our
civilization is doomed.

UNTHANKFUL

Although we celebrate Thanksgiving Day every year, our
affluent society knows nothing about the thankful spirit of the
pilgrims. By comparison with ourselves, they had nothing to
be thankful for, yet they were thankful. Our society has been
so spoiled that it has taken for granted the unprecedented
blessings of this land. Our forefathers were thankful for life,
liberty, and the chance to earn their livelihood freely. We have

enjoyed more freedom, education, and material possessions than any country in history, yet we are a nation of ungrateful gripers.

The grumbling of Americans in the face of plenty extends from the cradle to the grave. Children are unappreciative of sacrifices made by their parents, and parents tend to complain about the confining responsibilities of parenthood. The best-paid workers in the world are often more irked at the profits of their employers than they are grateful for the high economic standards provided them. Even senior citizens who in other cultures rarely live to enjoy their retirement gripe about having nothing to do.

I am not suggesting that this country is perfect — she has many failings, certainly — but anyone who has traveled throughout the world must acknowledge that ours is the best country on earth, probably the best that has ever existed. Yet we are plagued with the disease of ingratitude.

Unthankful people are never happy people. This is one area where Christians have a wonderful opportunity to witness to the reality of their faith. Spirit-filled Christians are always thankful (Ephesians 5:18-21), and thankful people are mentally healthy people doing the will of God (1 Thessalonians 5:18). Believers should shine as bright lights in this ungrateful generation!

UNHOLY

The animalistic philosophy of our society has produced an unholy, irreligious society. Only a small percentage of people today attend church regularly to study the Word of God, and an even smaller percentage try to live holy lives. We have reduced our strong Christian heritage, in which Sunday was almost universally respected, to a working,

buying, playing, desecrated day. Not that going to church
every Sunday makes you a Christian, but usually what people
do in relation to God on Sunday, "The Lord's day," sets a precedent for their activities the rest of the week.

WITHOUT NATURAL AFFECTION

Child abandonment violates one of the basic instincts of
motherhood, yet repeatedly newspapers carry the story of
neglected children, thus testifying to this increasing tendency.
In recent years our shock at child neglect has given rise to
complacency as we read of a beautiful little girl abandoned on
the dividing strip of a busy freeway, or a mother who watches
her second husband stomp to death her son of the first marriage. We say, "They are sick." Yes, they are heart-sick, for
they are "without natural affection."

Next to the desire for survival, one of man's most natural
desires is love for a member of the opposite sex. God has put
this strong drive within us for the purpose of propagation.
We are witnessing a decline in this desire by many and a
substitution of lust for one's own sex in homosexuality and
lesbianism. In fact, it is reaching epidemic proportions as its
participants, driven by perverted affection, are boldly calling
for its legalization.

The most disgraceful advocate of homosexuality I have
seen was a so-called minister who, dressed in clerical robes
and blasphemously clutching a cross, set up a communion
table on the City Hall steps in San Diego and proclaimed
a six-day fast to attract attention to his cause. This sexual
perversion, along with many others, is another evidence of
the growing lack of natural affection predicted for the last
days.

TRUCE BREAKERS, FALSE ACCUSERS

"My word is my bond" used to be a common expression in
the days when Christian principles prevailed in this country.
Today, even when an agreement is established in writing, we
can't be sure that some clever lawyer won't so twist things
that truth is circumvented.

Nations and governments can no longer be trusted, as
illustrated by Russia. Since 1933 when this nation officially
recognized the Communist regime in Russia, we have made
fifty-two treaties with them. So far they have broken fifty-
one! Our own country's leaders have lied to us on occasion as
well as to the rest of the world.

When deceit is uncovered, whether individual or corporate,
the guilty party's tendency is to accuse someone else of the very
thing he is doing. Israel and Egypt have broadcast false accusa-
tions so consistently that it will be impossible to get an accurate
record for history. In short, this is the day of declining integrity,
another predicted characteristic of the last days.

INCONTINENT, FIERCE, DESPISERS

Three characteristics of the last days can be linked together
due to their interrelated nature. The Greek word for *incontinent* means "without power of self-control." This suggests
a self-indulgent generation, which fits our society perfectly.
Incontinency breeds the "fierce" spirit of men today, a
matter which will be dealt with more specifically in the
next chapter.

TRAITORS

Not many years ago traitors were very few. Aaron Burr and
Benedict Arnold were the only known traitors in American

history for almost a century, but in recent years hundreds of men and women have joined them in infamy. We have been amazed to hear of American scientists who reveal atomic secrets to our enemies, high government officials who disclose our plans to the Communists, double agents who betray both sides, hundreds of young men who burn their draft cards or emigrate to Sweden, and many prominent professors or leading citizens who advocate the overthrow of our government by force and violence. Who could deny that we are living in a day of traitors?

HEADSTRONG OR RECKLESS

The word translated *heady* literally means a headstrong person who is led by passion into reckless living. He does not count the cost of his actions, but impulsively rushes ahead. This is the story of our day. Whether it is rushing to the marriage altar, buying a house we can ill afford, spending money, leaping to life-molding decisions, or just driving a car, most people live recklessly today.

HIGH-MINDED

One Greek scholar suggests that this Greek word means "to raise a smoke, to wrap in a mist. It is used metaphorically, to make proud, puff up with pride, render insolent."[2] This word certainly describes the unsaved intellectual community whose concepts are based on humanism. Blind to the fact that they are leading the world governmentally, socially, economically, and just about every other way into chaos, they smugly think of themselves as the "illuminated ones" surrounded by the ignorant masses. If you think that an exaggeration, then you should go with me to the college campus to debate such individuals and note their response when they discover you are a fundamentalist minister of the gospel. Their attitude strongly suggests intellectual conceit, certainly a form of "high-mindedness."

PLEASURE LOVERS

Like the Romans before us, we are a society of "lovers of pleasures more than lovers of God." The demonic enemy of man knows that one way to keep men from waking up to the disastrous days ahead is to occupy their minds with exciting nonessentials.

In recent years we have witnessed an amazing fascination for sports — in fact, most population centers have no respite. Baseball season isn't over before football begins, followed by basketball, hockey, track, boxing, and other sports. Billions are spent annually on this entertainment.

Sports for the most part are clean, whereas many forms of entertainment are downright immoral. Go-go shops featuring topless or bottomless dancers that once shocked a community are now commonplace, and we ask ourselves, "How can it get much worse?" But it will.

POWERLESS FORMALISM

"Having a form of godliness, but denying the power of it," offers a perfect description of many of the major Protestant denominations and the Catholic Church. They stress form and ceremony, but as we saw concerning apostasy and the ecumenical church, they are powerless. They have power to influence legislation, direct social reform, and create civil unrest, but they are powerless when it comes to introducing men to the transforming power of Jesus Christ. For the most part, they

"deny the power" — that is, they no longer believe he is supernatural. Consequently, they have no power with God. Like
Samson of old, today's liberal religious leaders are unaware
that "the Lord has departed from them."

The eighteen characteristics of the perilous times predicted
for "the last days" read like the daily newspaper. Hardly a day
goes by in which we do not read or hear about some event
that further illustrates the perilous times God predicted, giving
further evidence that we are living in the last days and that
Christ's coming cannot be delayed much longer.

THE CHRISTIAN

It would be a mistake not to call attention to the fact that this
passage of Scripture closes with a challenge to Christians with
regard to living in these perilous times. We are told: "From
such turn away." It is a mistake for the Christian to think he
can fellowship closely with the covetous, blasphemers, proud,
disobedient, unthankful, and unholy and not be influenced by
them. For that reason we are instructed to turn away from
them. We may offer spiritual help, but we are not to partake of
their sins. Keep in mind, the lowering standards of the world
do not change the holy standards of God.

1. Norman B. Harrison, *His Sure Return* (Minneapolis: Harrison Service, 1952),
   p. 39.
2. Kenneth S. Wuest, *The Pastoral Epistles in the Greek New Testament* (Grand Rapids: Eerdmans, 1952), p. 144.

ELEVEN
A FLOOD OF WICKEDNESS

"And as it was in the days of Noah, so shall it be also in the days of the Son of man. They did eat, they drank, they married wives, they were given in marriage, until the day that Noah entered into the ark, and the flood came, and destroyed them all. Likewise also as it was in the days of Lot; they did eat, they drank, they bought, they sold, they planted, they builded; but the same day that Lot went out of Sodom it rained fire and brimstone from heaven, and destroyed them all. Even thus shall it be in the day when the Son of man is revealed" (Luke 17:26-30).

Twice in history mankind became so corrupt that God visited them with catastrophic judgment. We may find similar devastation in history, as in the volcanic destruction of Pompeii, but these had no heavenly denunciation. We do not wonder why the flood destroyed the world's population except for eight people in the days of Noah, or why Sodom and Gomorrah were consumed in the days of Lot. The Bible makes it very clear: the people were so evil that God's mercy was exhausted and in his holiness he "destroyed them all."

The Lord Jesus singled out these two judgments as illustrations of conditions on the earth just prior to his Second Coming. If you follow through on the illustrations, you recognize that immediately after Jesus' return to take his Church out of the world, the world will be plunged into judgment doom comparable to those historic days of catastrophe.

Since our Lord predicted mankind's return to the conditions that caused those two great judgments, it would be helpful to examine the Bible carefully to discover what they were. Such an examination reveals that four degenerating conditions pervaded the days of Noah and Lot. You will have to decide for yourself whether or not you can see history repeating itself.

SEXUAL PERVERSION

One of the most beautiful and meaningful relationships that two people of the opposite sex can share is the oneness of physical union, properly called "the act of marriage." God meant this experience both for the propagation of the human race and the emotional enrichment and physical pleasure of a husband and wife. Contrary to popular opinion, it is a sacred and holy experience in the eyes of God when confined to marriage. God places prohibitions on the sex act only outside of marriage. In fact, the Bible makes it very clear that God considers any form of sex outside of the marriage relationship a perversion of sex.

Sexual perversion was rampant in the days of both Noah and Lot. Genesis 6:1-2 indicates a mixing of marriage between the godly line and the human line — a violation of the will of God (verse 3). Our Lord's indication that there were days of "marrying and giving in marriage" (Matthew 24:38) suggests to many Bible teachers that it was a time of mixed marriages of short duration, similar to the rampant marriage and divorce trends of our day.

The repugnant story of Lot in Sodom was even worse. Not only was there a breakdown in marriage and the home, but homosexuality was prevalent. The Bible says of the Sodomites (a name used for centuries to describe sexual perversion) that "their sin is very grievous" (Genesis 18:20). The story narrated here reveals the depths of depravity to which man can sink when he rejects God. We stand amazed at men so evil as to demand sexual relations with men and refuse virgin women. But the apostle Paul describes how such conditions developed.

"Because that, when they knew God, they glorified him not as God, neither were thankful; but became vain in their imaginations, and their foolish heart was darkened. Professing themselves to be wise, they became fools, and changed the glory of the uncorruptible God into an image made like to corruptible man, and to birds, and four-footed beasts, and creeping things. Wherefore God also gave them up to uncleanness through the lusts of their own hearts, to dishonor their own bodies between themselves; who changed the truth of God into a lie, and worshiped and served the creature more than the Creator, who is blessed forever. For this cause God gave them up unto vile affections; for even their women did change the natural use into that which is against nature, and likewise also the men, leaving the natural use of the woman, burned in their lust one toward another, men with men working that which is unseemly, and receiving in themselves that recompence of their error which was meet. And even as they did not like to retain God in their knowledge, God gave them over to a reprobate mind, to do those things which are not convenient" (Romans 1:21-28).

Who can deny that we are living in corrupt days like those

of Noah and Lot? The greatest single problem of our society is the nationwide breakdown of the home and the soaring divorce rate that in some places destroys one in two marriages. A newspaper report indicated that California's easy divorce laws increased the divorce rate 40 percent in its first six months.

Sexual promiscuity has been proposed and practiced by free-love advocates of our society until men and women mate like animals, and wonder why they feel like beasts.

A thirty-one-year-old woman told a doctor friend of mine that she had experienced relations with so many different men she couldn't begin to count them. "I'm sure it's at least one hundred," she disclosed. No wonder he was treating her for venereal disease, which is presently a strong indication of widespread promiscuity. In spite of the V.D. "cure-all," penicillin, syphilis and gonorrhea cases have reached epidemic proportions, according to the San Diego Health Department. In three years their treatment load has jumped from just over one thousand cases annually to over seven thousand, and now they have discovered a V.D. strain that resists penicillin.

In the last few years the sensibilities of decent people have been shocked as homosexuality has come out of its closet and arrogantly paraded itself on the stage of the U.S. Congress, where two self-acknowledged homosexuals have been reelected to Congress—one after being rebuked by the House "Ethics" committee after having sex with a sixteen-year-old page. The other was reelected after publicly admitting to having a long term sexual relation with a notorious homosexual prostitute who ran a prostitution den out of the congressman's home in Washington, D.C. Recently homosexuals have been granted marriage licenses in San Francisco, and are determined not to rest until they are officially acknowledged as "a family" and authorized to adopt children throughout the nation. They have come a long way since Moses was commanded by God to have them stoned!

Today the homosexual movement is one of the most powerful political forces in the country. AIDS is the only governmentally protected plague in the nation thanks to the intimidating power of the homosexual lobby. No other disease bearer is given so much freedom to infect other people. Rather than embarrass AIDS carriers, they are not subject to contact tracing like other infectious disease carriers, yet AIDS is always fatal. AIDS research has gained more government funding in a shorter period of time than any other disease in history, thanks to the homosexual lobby. It was less than fifteen years ago that a Canadian flight attendant brought AIDS into this country and already twenty-five thousand people have died of it and several million are suspected of being HIV positive, most of whom will contract the disease in three to seven years. And instead of demanding typical health precautions required of other communicable diseases like TB, polio, smallpox, etc., our government protects homosexuals. Insanity? No — just the greed on behalf of liberal politicians to stay in office. Most know that if the homosexual voters turned against them, they would lose in the next election.

This is an indictment on the church! If we voted in the same percentage as the homosexual community (about 85 percent while evangelical Christians voted 40.5 percent in 1990) homosexual-protecting liberal politicians would be voted out of office in six years or less. (Most congressional and senatorial elections are won by a margin of 1 to 8 or 9 percent; consequently, a strong group voting en masse like homosexuals, who only make up 6 to 8 percent of the population, are often a significant voting force way out of proportion to their numbers. The trouble is, homosexuals understand that — Christians don't.) History shows that no nation can long endure the legal acceptance of homosexuality. Many feel that the current AIDS epidemic is a judgment from God — and who can say conclusively that it is not? Hopefully the Christian community will wake up to the seriousness of this plague and vote homosexually lenient politicians out of office. Perhaps it will take more tragedies like the Christian heart surgeon who is dying of AIDS at forty. Even though he has never had a homosexual experience, he caught the dread disease from a patient he operated on in 1985. The hospital thought more of the AIDS patient than they did of the doctor for they never told him of the patient's condition. Now a Christian wife and five children are without a father and husband. Sooner or later our government is going to have to start caring more for the healthy instead of protecting the perverted from the consequences of their evil life-style.

EVIL IMAGINATIONS

"And God saw that the wickedness of man was great in the earth, and that every imagination of the thoughts of his heart was only evil continually" (Genesis 6:5).

This depravity of Noah's day scarcely needs further confirmation as a characteristic of our present generation. We described it in our earlier chapter, "Perilous Times." It will suffice here to point out the cause for this gross wickedness. As a man "thinketh in his heart, so is he" (Proverbs 23:7). Not since the days preceding the French Revolution has Western civilization been inundated by such an avalanche of pornographic filth. Erotic pictures and sordid sex novels are openly advertised in book stores from coast to coast. Movies have reached an all-time low in morals, for promiscuity and infidelity have given place to lesbianism, homosexuality, incest, and every depraved imagination of man.

Pornography is no longer the property of a few degenerate crea-
tures, but is the mental diet of millions. Evil thoughts fan the
imaginations of young and old, consuming moral standards and
restraints, just as in the wicked days before the flood and the
destruction of Sodom and Gomorrah.

A trip through Europe convinced me that America does not
have a monopoly on pornography products, for it is even
worse on that continent. You can hardly buy a newspaper
from a stand without facing large displays of magazines with
covers showing vile sex acts in living color.

I purposely left the previous two sentences from the 1972
version of this book to let you see how far we have degenerated in two decades. Little did I know then that the 1972
Ginsberg case on pornography would open the floodgates of
this country to the present porno-plague. On a vote of seven
liberals to two, this decision did away with two hundred years
of traditional standards upholding decent literature, until we
are now the pornographic capital of the world. Dr. James
Dobson, who served on the Attorney General's commission
on pornography, found this $10 billion industry is controlled
largely by the Mafia. It is also a national disgrace that the violent rape and child molestation increase in this country is in
direct parallel to the increase in the production of pornography. In the last five years, pornography has taken over television production and that media vehicle to the mind is even
more powerful than print porn, for it excites "evil imaginations" like nothing else in our society. This powerful form of
mental perversion is fulfilling prophecy.

A VIOLENT SOCIETY

"And God looked upon the earth, and behold, it was corrupt . . . and God said . . . , The earth is filled with violence

through them; and, behold, I will destroy them with the earth"
(Genesis 6:12-13).

As you compare this description with that of Lot's day, you
will note that both generations produced lovers of violence.
Whenever men degenerate sexually to the level of animals,
they also adopt the animalistic propensity for violence.

The peaceful, law-abiding citizens who once marked our
culture were nurtured by laws and principles laid down by our
Christian forefathers. These laws have given place to "progressive ideas" based on atheistic humanism; consequently, we are
living in a violent society. The evolutionist, convinced that
man's behavior is due to his environment, has determined to
protect criminals from oppressive society at the expense of
law-abiding citizens, rendering city streets unsafe.

Every day our newspapers report the tragic parade of
violence. Accounts of rapings, stabbings, mayhem, and murder are the real-life acts of violence children have watched
casually on TV for the past forty years. Washington, D.C., is
one of the most unsafe cities in the world. A U.S. senator's
wife was stabbed in a Washington park in broad daylight,
and even armed guards have not been able to guarantee
safety to the secretaries who work in congressional office
buildings. From New York to Los Angeles we continually
witness havoc and death. This lenient attitude toward criminals has resulted in graphic reductions in penalties, endless
paperwork, and restrictions on police, rendering our city
streets hotbeds of crime, drugs, and prostitution, but unsafe
for law-abiding citizens.

An article on violence in *U.S. News and World Report* indicated that raging brutality is not limited to America. Accounts
of similar violence in Tokyo, New Delhi, London, Paris, Rome,
and cities in Africa and South America dramatized our plight.
At no time in the past twenty-five years have we been free from

the existence of war somewhere in the world, and in this past quarter of a century millions of people have died by violence. While the world is not yet filled with violence, it is shuddering and bleeding before a loving God who may be nearing the end of his patience — as in the days of Noah and Lot!

CASUAL LIVING

In spite of the preaching of Noah and the warnings of Lot, people went right on eating, drinking, buying, selling, marrying, and giving in marriage until the flood came or the brimstone fell. Obviously, there was nothing wrong in these activities, for they are a part of everyday life. And that is the point. The people of Noah's and Lot's day continued to live ordinary lives in the face of impending disaster. They refused to believe the warnings of God.

Today the Word of God cries out to unrighteous men to repent of their destructive self-will and make Jesus Christ the Lord and Savior of their lives, but the whispers of Satan seem much louder and clearer. The prophecies of Scripture clearly indicate that the coming of Christ may be at any time, but only a few pay heed. Instead, the world rushes about, buying, selling, eating, drinking, marrying, and giving in marriage. This generation, as the Lord predicted, is like Noah's generation, which "knew not until the flood came, and took them all away; so shall also the coming of the Son of man be" (Matthew 24:39).

HARK, THE ARK!

Several years ago while preaching on this subject, I made the following statement: "There is nothing in the Bible that requires God to reveal the whereabouts of Noah's ark and the ruins of Sodom and Gomorrah, but I wouldn't be surprised if he did." My reasoning was simply this: since God is a revealer of himself to men, and since he likened the generation of the last days to that of Noah and Lot, I wouldn't be surprised if he gave the world additional, special evidence that his Word is true.

There are few events in the Bible that have been so consistently ridiculed as the flood and the destruction of Lot's cities. The reason is twofold. Skeptics do not like to acknowledge the supernatural element in the Bible, and both of these events require the supernatural power of God. In addition, these two historic events demonstrate that God punishes sinful men. Unbelievers detest the thought of a God who would punish lawbreakers. They much prefer thinking the Bible is only words, whereas the discovery of Noah's ark and Sodom and Gomorrah would suggest the wages of sin might be death after all!

Please bear in mind that I am not predicting the discovery of these things, but merely suggesting the possibility. After all, their discovery would not make them more factual than their inclusion in the Bible and their mention by the Lord Jesus Christ; but it would shake up the doubters!

With this in mind, you can imagine my excitement in August 1968, when, while leading a tour to the Holy Land, I heard the Jewish tour guide say as he pointed to the southern shore of the Dead Sea, "This is the site of the ancient city of Sodom, destroyed by fire and brimstone." Naturally, we asked a host of questions! "Much of the rock you see around here is brimstone. There is also much salt." He facetiously added, "In fact, that pillar over there may be Lot's wife." Frankly, it didn't look much like the woman who disobeyed the heavenly warning and looked back on the burning cities, but there were several pillars of salt in the area. Like other tourists, I hopped off the bus and picked up a rock sure enough, it was solid salt!

Back in Jerusalem I gained some additional information. It seems that two American skin divers swore they discovered buildings in the water at the south end of the Dead Sea. Their attempts to take underwater pictures of the structures proved fruitless due to the exceedingly high salt content, but they claimed they could feel building blocks under the water that were entirely man made and foreign to the surrounding terrain. It is a well-recognized fact that the Dead Sea is many miles longer to the south than it was in ancient times. Therefore, there may be truth in the conviction of the Jews today that Sodom was located there and its buildings now lie under brimstone and water.

In the fall of 1969, I read about a man who was trying to organize an expedition to Mount Ararat in eastern Turkey to search for Noah's ark. I wrote to him, explaining that I was an author and student of Bible prophecy and would very much like to accompany him on his expedition in order to write up the account of the ark's discovery. He graciously answered my letter and invited me to his home in Farmington, New Mexico. Unfortunately, the expedition did not materialize due to lack of financing, but I found Eryl Cummings one of the most fascinating people I have ever met.

For twenty-five years this man had followed every clue or rumor about sightings of Noah's ark at a personal expense in excess of $100,000. He opened to me his fifteen volumes of research materials, painstakingly arranged by him and his wife, Violet.

Consider the following, which is the essence of Cumming's research.

1840—An earthquake, which blew out one-tenth of the upper peak of Mount Ararat, inundated the little town of Ahora. After this, explorers began to report sightings of the ark.

1856—An Armenian guide, his son, and three English atheists found the ark, but the atheists bound themselves to a "death oath" rather than admit to the discovery. The boy migrated to America and told his incredible story; years later one of the atheists admitted his part in the plot in a deathbed confession.

1883—London newspapers carried the story of a group of Turkish commissioners who were appointed to investigate an avalanche on the mountain. Their explorations revealed the ark buried in an iceberg. According to their report, they chiseled the ice away from three rooms and found it to be an immense ship.

1887—Prince Nouri, archdeacon of Babylon and the apostolic leader of the Nestorians, climbed the mountain three times and said he stood awed and overwhelmed as he saw the old ark there, wedged in between two rocks and half filled with snow and ice. He claimed that he entered the rooms and found them in agreement with the scriptural account.

1916—A Russian air force pilot reported seeing the ship on a test flight over Mount Ararat. A report was sent to the czar, who dispatched two parties of soldiers in search of the ark. Both groups viewed, photographed, and measured the ark. A courier was sent to the czar with the report, but while he was en route the Communists overthrew the government and the courier was never heard from. This story, first revealed to the Christian world in 1945 but later discounted for lack of corroboration, is what started Eryl Cummings on his quest for Noah's ark. He has since confirmed the story through at least five independent witnesses and reports.

1917—Five Turkish soldiers returning home from Baghdad after the war decided to go by way of Mount Ararat. They told essentially the same story as others—of seeing the great ship encased in ice high in the mountains.

1943—Stars and Stripes, the G.I. newspaper of World War II, carried the story of two air force pilots who flew the air route from Ervan, Russia, to Tunisia over the mountains of Ararat, claiming they saw a large ship in a small lake high in the mountains. A Russian major also claimed to have seen such a ship.

1948—Reshit, a Kurdish farmer, professed to have climbed up the mountain and found a large ship so hard that his knife would not cut into it.

1954—Thirty people swore that they saw eight photographs taken by George J. Greene of Corpus Christi, Texas, when he was on a mining expedition in the Ararat region. These pictures, taken from a helicopter, were of a large ship surrounded by ice. Unfortunately, Greene was killed in British Guiana, and the photos have never been found.

1955—Fernand Navarra, a French explorer, claims that he and his son found Noah's ark. He not only found the large shape of the ark buried under clear ice, but he chopped out a piece of hand-hewn timber nine inches by nine inches by five feet, which he cut from a much larger piece. He claims that there were many other timbers in the area weighing many tons. As Navarra, who is in the industrial wrecking business in Paris, asks, "What else could it be, 14,500 feet up on a mountain, 150 miles from the nearest tree, but Noah's ark?" The first carbon testing reports of Navarra's wood indicated it was possibly forty-five hundred years old. After scientists learned that it might be from Noah's ark, their later reports indicated a more recent age. Could it be they are afraid to face the truth? Two other Englishmen, Sir James Bryce and Hardwickie Knight, have found wood on the mountain, far from any buildings or the timberline.[1]

Since that time, there have been no actual sightings of the ark, even though several teams have searched carefully. Two men in particular, Dr. John Morris of the Institute for Creation Research and Jim Irwin, famous for being the first American spaceman to walk on the moon, have been there several times. Both are convinced it is up there and plan to return when Turkish government policy and continuous warm weather permit. One reason it has been so difficult to find is the high precipitation level during the past two decades, which could very well keep it hidden under massive tons of snow and ice — until God himself chooses to so arrange continuous years of warm climate so that the melt down will expose that mighty old vessel which would force scientists and evolutionists to rethink their favorite "science fiction" belief in the theory of evolution.

In the meantime however, when these stories are weighed in the light of many other reports, it is not so difficult to believe that Noah built a giant ship, the size of a modern aircraft carrier, that came to rest "on the mountains of Ararat," just as the Bible says, and that it may still be there.

But we do not have to hear an astounding announcement authenticate the truth of the Bible. Jesus has proved his reality and power to all who have carefully examined the "infallible proofs" of his resurrection from the dead. Since he is God and he referred to the fact that Noah was indeed a character of history who built an ark to save all forms of life — we know the ark existed thousands of years ago.

Hopefully God will reveal it soon as one more evidence to the faithfulness of his Word.

1. If you desire additional information or have knowledge of similar reports, please write to the Institute for Creation Research, P.O. Box 2667, El Cajon, CA 92021.

TWELVE
SCOFFERS HAVE COME

"This second epistle, beloved, I now write unto you, in both which I stir up your pure minds by way of remembrance, that ye may be mindful of the words which were spoken before by the holy prophets, and of the commandment of us, the apostles of the Lord the Savior; knowing this first, that there shall come in the last days scoffers, walking after their own lusts, and saying, Where is the promise of his coming? For since the fathers fell asleep, all things continue as they were from the beginning of the creation. For this they willingly are ignorant of, that by the word of God the heavens were of old, and the earth standing out of the water and in the water, whereby the world that then was, being overflowed with water, perished. But the heavens and the earth which are now, by the same word are kept in store, reserved unto fire against the day of judgment and perdition of ungodly men.

"But, beloved, be not ignorant of this one thing, that one day is with the Lord as a thousand years, and a thousand years as one day. The Lord is not slack concerning his promise, as some men count slackness, but is longsuffering to us-ward, not willing that any should perish, but that all should come to repentance. But the day of the Lord will come as a thief in the night, in which the heavens shall pass away with a great noise, and the elements shall melt with fervent heat, the earth also, and the works that are therein, shall be burned up. Seeing, then, that all these things shall be dissolved, what manner of persons ought ye to be in all holy conversation and godliness, looking for and hasting unto the coming of the day of God, in which the heavens, being on fire, shall be dissolved, and the elements shall melt with fervent heat?" (2 Peter 3:1-12).

One of the most interesting signs of our Lord's return, when considered in the light of contemporary thought, is the apostle Peter's suggestion that scoffers would come on the scene in the last days. Christianity has never lacked for scoffers, but today we seem to have more than ever before and they hold key positions of influence. If you deny that, try to get a major publisher to consider science books supporting biblical creationism rather than evolutionary theory; or attempt to get it reviewed by a major TV network. The molders of our educational and philosophic thought today are predominantly scoffers, acting exactly as the Bible predicted they would in the last days.

UNIFORMITARIAN SCOFFERS

Don't let that big word *uniformitarian* throw you. It simply means that the present uniform processes of life are sufficient to account for the origin and development of all the earth's physical and biological phenomena. This, of course, eliminates the necessity of divine revelation of catastrophic events designed by God to judge his creature, man.

This theory of uniformitarianism, popularized in the mid-1800s by the English geologist Sir Charles Lyell, became a prominent foundation for Darwinism and evolution, Marxism and socialism, Freudianism and liberalism. In fact, it fostered many of the evils that beset our society today, and it is propagated by the most intellectually trained members of our culture.

What is fascinating to us in this study is that almost two thousand years ago the apostle Peter, an untrained Galilean fisherman, predicted the exact thinking pattern that would characterize these scoffers. He prophesied that in the last days scoffers would come, denying the coming of Christ because "since the fathers fell asleep, all things continue as they were from the beginning of the creation" (2 Peter 3:4). That is exactly the philosophy of our day! "Gradual progression" from a spontaneous beginning through millions of years to the present order of things reflects the concept of the evolution-ists. The moment one suggests a catastrophic interruption in their theory of uniformity, they scoff.

The questions Peter said they would ask are based on their uniform ideas. If you eliminate the biblical worldwide Flood, as uniformitarians do, you remove a vital proof for the Second Coming of Christ. If there was in fact a Flood, then God judges sinful men and he will come again to judge the world. Therefore, if man accepts the reality of the Flood, he is pressed to accept the likelihood of Christ's Second Coming.

If you think I am suggesting that the intellectual com-munity is guilty of bias against the record in the Word of God, you are right! Dr. Henry Morris, a prolific writer who holds a Ph.D. in the field of hydraulics and headed the engineering department at Virginia Polytechnic Institute, shared the plight of geologist Clifford Burdick with a graduate school president. The University of Arizona had refused to confer a Ph.D. degree on Burdick, an out-standing student, because of an article he wrote in favor of creationism. (He later received the degree from the

University of Physical Science at Phoenix.) Dr. Morris asked his colleague if V.P.I. would confer a doctorate on a straight-A graduate student who knew the evolutionary theory thoroughly and was well qualified in every respect but did not believe in evolution. The president became tense and with no small emotion replied, "Absolutely not!" Now, I ask you—does that sound like intellectual objectivity?

BLINDNESS OF SCOFFERS

With superb logic, Peter tells us why our contemporary intellectuals are blind to the truth of creation by the direct act of God—so blind, in fact, that in the name of science they become unscientific. As we have seen, the whole assumption of uniformitarianism is that ". . . all things continue as they were from the beginning." If that assumption can be disproved, the entire theory must be discarded. Dr. Morris and many other scholarly scientists from every known field of science believe this is possible.[1]

Besides being contradicted by the second law of thermodynamics, the Ice Age (for which the uniformitarians have no adequate explanation), population growth, and other factors, uniformitarianism is diametrically opposed to the Word of God. Peter points out that the Bible record makes the entire theory of uniformity invalid. To see this graphically, examine the chart on pages 158–159.

KEPT BY THE WORD OF GOD

Five major historical events appear in the Bible.

Creation: God was the originator of all things, including man.

The Fall of man: Sometime shortly after creation man

chose to disobey God and fell from innocence into sin. Death, disease, and human misery resulted.

The Flood: Man's iniquity reached such depths that God destroyed all but eight people in the world's greatest cataclysm, the Flood.

The Life of Christ: Jesus Christ came to die as a divine sacrifice for man's sin, to lift the curse on man, and prepare man for a future state of bliss where he could enjoy the unlimited blessings originally intended for him by his Creator.

Second Coming of Christ: This will be the fifth major event in God's plan for man; as we are seeing, it apparently is in the near future.

According to Peter's argument, the scoffers are thoroughly mistaken in their notion that things have continued in a state of uniformity. To the contrary, man has seen two major divisions of time and there is a third to come. The first, which was terminated by the Flood, is called by Peter "the world that then was." The present world he calls "the heavens and the earth that now are." The third, after the Second Coming of Christ, will provide a new heaven and earth, all of which are kept in place by the word (or power) of God.

Peter very clearly teaches that this world has undergone one earthshaking catastrophe and will experience yet another. The first one, the Flood of Noah's day, changed the order of nature in the atmosphere and on the earth. Consequently, the present order is not sufficiently similar to the one before the Flood to provide us with accurate indications of what that world was like. Scientists who draw conclusions from present conditions and apply them to different conditions before the Flood arrive inevitably at wrong conclusions. This makes the discovery of Noah's Ark potentially important in the Bible's case against evolutionary humanism.

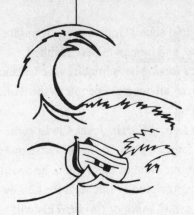

CREATION

THE FLOOD

AGES PAST

CATASTROPHE

"THE WORLD THAT WAS"
v. 6

"THE WORLD

KEPT BY THE

**CHRIST'S
FIRST COMING**

**THE SECOND
COMING**

AGES
TO
COME

MILLENNIUM

DAY OF THE LORD

THAT NOW IS"
v. 7

"NEW HEAVENS & NEW EARTH"
vv. 10-13

WORD OF GOD . . . 2 Peter 3:1-14

WHY ARE THEY SO BLIND?

When confronted with the growing evidence against uniformitarianism, some of it supplied by non-Christian scholars such as Hapgood, Hooker, Sanderson, and Velikovsky, many people wonder why scoffers are so blind. The apostle Peter provides us with two reasons.

The first is found in 1 Peter 3:5: "For this they are willingly ignorant of." It is difficult for a student who trusts his professor to realize that his teacher may be seriously prejudiced, but such is often true! The professor's bias may not be caused only by repeating thoughts that were systematized and handed to him by his teachers with little critical scrutiny, but by a mental block at the outset. The unregenerated minds of unbelievers resist the idea of the intervention of God in human affairs. Intellectuals pride themselves in being objective, but objectivity suffers when non-Christians encounter the Word of God. The problem is spiritual — a matter of the will — and the unbeliever is deliberately ignorant of the truth.

A great American whom I deeply admire came to our city on a speaking engagement. I wrote ahead and invited him to have breakfast with me. As we ate, I shared with him the concern of my heart. "How is it that you have escaped liberalism in the fields of economics, government, history, philosophy, and education, but have swallowed it in the area of religion?" He replied, "I settled the matter forty years ago on the subject of origins; I believe man is the product of evolution." "But there have been amazing discoveries in geology, anthropology, archaeology, and other fields that discredit evolution," I said. With a voice of steel he announced: "The matter is closed!" Here is a man who can carefully weigh the evidence in worldly matters, but his mind is closed to spiritual realities. Is the problem lack of evidence? Oh, no: "Willingly ignorant!"

Long before geologist Lyell promoted his theory of

uniformitarianism, he was an atheistic humanist. As such, he rejected the biblical record. It is not surprising that he would arrive at conclusions diametrically opposed to the teachings of the Bible. Nor should we be surprised that Lyell's uniformitarianism, rejected by men like Pasteur, was accepted readily and advanced by the humanists of his day. All had one thing in common: they were "willingly ignorant" of the truth of God's Word.

Another reason for their intellectual blindness, frequently overlooked, is mentioned by Peter in verse 3. During the last days scoffers will come, "walking after their own lusts." The lovers of pleasure and plunder who foster the "free love" movement, advocate the use of marijuana, and lead rebellions against society are bosom friends of uniformitarian philosophy! If we would learn from history instead of ignoring it, we would remember that the early humanists lived that way.

Voltaire and Rousseau, two French skeptics who had no small influence in the development of humanism, were moral degenerates. I have often wondered if college students' admiration for this "free spirit" would continue if they realized that Rousseau's mistress bore him five illegitimate children whom he callously abandoned at the Paris General Hospital.[2]

All the evidence in the world — scientific and rational — will not convince the man who, like the Pharisee of Jesus' day, "willed not to come" to him. Nor can a man bent on pleasure hear the voice of the Spirit. Only when such a person comes to the end of himself will he seek the real and ultimate truth. Fortunately, many casualties of the scoffers are still open to truth. For these we should be available daily to the Holy Spirit to share with them the promises of God.

TWENTIETH-CENTURY SCOFFERS

Throughout this study I have tried to show that each sign of our Lord's return has its roots in the First World War or events following that conflagration. That is difficult to maintain in this case because uniformitarianism became influential in the nineteenth century. But not until after World War I did the theory become dogma for American educators. And through educators the theory of uniformitarian evolution became the gospel of humanism for American students.

Prior to the Great War, three schools produced most of the teachers of America. They were Harvard, Princeton, and Yale, schools that were originally founded to train ministers and missionaries to preach the gospel of Christ. In the early 1920s, John Dewey and his progressive education (based on uniformitarianism) made Columbia University the new headquarters for training educators. Although many Bible-believing Christians teach in the public schools today, the overwhelming majority of teachers indoctrinate their students with the evolutionary uniformitarian misconception as the force and control of all life.

While I was gathering material for my book *How To Be Happy Though Married,* an experience occurred that shows how things have changed since the First World War. While reading a book on physical relations in marriage, written by one of the leaders of the school of medicine at the University of Chicago, I found high moral principles and biblical standards advocated by the author. Turning to the front, I found it was copyrighted in 1921. It has been just about that long since the University of Chicago or any other secular school forthrightly propounded biblical concepts. Uniformitarian thought has supplanted biblical convictions in the academic world!

During the past two decades we have witnessed an antimoral assault on the minds of our youth by some of the most highly educated atheists in our country. They have inundated the minds of 45 million school children with massive amounts of radically explicit sex education taught in mixed classes without benefit of moral values. Add to that "values clarification" — which is nothing more than a scientific assault on the moral values a child brings to school from his home or church — and death and dying education, global education — and the list goes on. These courses have created an obsession on sex in the minds of our young at a time when they need an obsession on learning. This has resulted in a wave of teenage sexual promiscuity unmatched in human history, a tripling of teen, unwed pregnancies from 300,000 a year in 1970 to over one million in 1990 and an unbelievable increase in sexually transmitted diseases — some of which were unknown two decades ago.

Thoughtful people are asking, "Why would an educated adult with a Ph.D. degree encourage fourteen- and fifteen-year-old children to practice their sexuality promiscuously as though they were animals?" The answer is simple — because they believe they are! These humanistic educators without moral values are committed evolutionists who follow the logic of their evolutionary beliefs — that since "there is no one up there telling you what is right or wrong," you're just an animal, so why not act sexually like the animal you are? As professor Alan Bloom, in his 1990 blockbusting best-seller, *The Closing of the American Mind,* pointed out, the relativistic attitude of our best educated youth today about morals is: "They are no big deal!" Such popular but erroneous thinking has resulted in the near death of virtue, millions of fatherless children, and millions of disease-plagued youth — much like the moral conditions described by the New Testament prophets for the coming Tribulation period, which may be close at hand. In fact, the present moral holocaust based as it is on an evolutionary philosophy that rejects God, creation, and moral absolutes is an exact fulfillment of this sign of end-time moral conditions. So bad are these moral conditions that it can be safely predicted that if this country does not soon experience a moral-spiritual revival of gigantic proportions, we will either fall into a national decline or usher in the Frankenstein-like conditions of the Tribulation period.

THE PROMISE OF GOD

Even a brief examination of Peter's prophecy would be deficient without a look at the promise of God in 1 Peter 3:7-15. Since the Bible clearly establishes the fact of a global Flood (which provides explanation for the Ice Age; the arctic regions that once were tropical in climate but are now inundated with ice; the perfectly preserved mammoths and other animals instantly frozen at temperatures of minus-150 F.; and fresh water icebergs floating in salt water oceans), we know that a world catastrophe separates our present world from a previous culture. This fact is used by Peter as a sign that such a catastrophe will end this present order and usher in a new one which he calls the new heavens and the new earth. He concludes that since creation, the Flood catastrophe, and the present world order were caused and sustained by God's word, so the future is guaranteed by his word, including the judgment of ungodly men (verse 7). In short, the Flood of Noah's day confirms both the coming of Christ and his judgment on unrepentant men.

ONE DAY — ONE THOUSAND YEARS

We tend to think that promises of short duration are more valid than long ones. That is because we are used to dealing with inconsistent human beings. With God it is quite different. Just because his promise to return for his Church is almost two thousand years old, we do not consider it an ancient promise! Actually, it is only "two days" old, and time does not depreciate the validity of God's promises. As Peter said, "The Lord is not slack concerning his promises, as some men count slackness." God keeps his promises. Christ *will* come again!

LIKE A THIEF HE WILL COME

Christ's coming will be unexpected by the masses; that is why it is compared to a thief who comes when we least expect him. Not since the early days of the Church have so many people been totally oblivious to the fact of Christ's coming. What a shock it will be!

"Seeing, then, that all these things shall be dissolved, what manner of persons ought ye to be in all holy conversation and godliness" (2 Peter 3:11). The times in which we live cry out to us for consecrated living. Because this world will be dissolved in a gigantic atomic explosion (not set off by man, but controlled by God), we ought to leave no stone unturned in our efforts to warn the lost to come to Christ.

THE WILL OF GOD

One final word is needed here concerning the will of God revealed in verse 9. "The Lord . . . is longsuffering toward us, not willing that any should perish, but that all should come to repentance." This verse, as clearly as any in the Bible, tells us of God's will for man. First, he doesn't want any man to perish who is willing to trust Christ; instead, he waits for all those who will be a part of the body of Christ to turn to him as Lord and Savior.

God has given us a free will. He desires each one to turn that will over to him voluntarily. He will never force us to do so. Instead, he speaks to us out of his Word and invites us to turn to him through his Son, Jesus Christ. Only the individual can make that decision.

Two kinds of people exist in the world today: those who have done the will of God, and those who have not. Have you obeyed God from the heart and turned your life over to Jesus Christ? If not, why don't you do it now?

The scoffers of our day would ridicule such a suggestion, but consider two things about them. First, their existence reminds us of Peter's prophecy about the last days. Second, the scoffers in Noah's day were disastrously wrong. Twenti-eth-century scoffers will fare no better!

1. If you are interested in studying this matter, I suggest you write to the Institute for Creation Research, P. O.Box 2667, El Cajon, CA, 92021, for a bibliography of excellent books on the subject.
2. *Grolier Encyclopedia,* Vol. 17 (1960), page 135.

THIRTEEN
THE ECUMENICAL CHURCH

"And there came one of the seven angels which had the seven vials, and talked with me, saying unto me: Come hither; I will show unto thee the judgment of the great whore that sitteth upon many waters, with whom the kings of the earth have committed fornication, and the inhabitants of the earth have been made drunk with the wine of her fornication. So he carried me away in the Spirit into the wilderness: and I saw a woman sit upon a scarlet-colored beast, full of names of blasphemy, having seven heads and ten horns. And the woman was arrayed in purple and scarlet color, and decked with gold and precious stones and pearls, having a golden cup in her hand, full of abominations and filthiness of her fornication; and upon her forehead was a name written: Mystery, Babylon the Great, The Mother of Harlots and Abominations of the Earth. And I saw the woman drunken with the blood of the saints, and with the blood of the martyrs of Jesus; and when I saw her, I wondered with great admiration" (Revelation 17:1-6).

Over thirty years ago my uncle, Dr. E. W. Palmer, who since has celebrated fifty years in the gospel ministry, was

pastor of a large church in Oak Park, Illinois. During some
services he held in our church in Minneapolis, I heard him
say, "One of the most dangerous movements in Christendom
today is the trend toward ecumenicity." I scratched my head
and wondered what he meant. After studying Bible prophecy
I quit wondering, for the Bible clearly foretells that during the
Tribulation period there will be one vast religious system — all
others will be amalgamated into it. Naturally, such a thing as
religious unity cannot take place overnight. It therefore must
begin prior to the Tribulation period. I submit that the modern
ecumenical movement is doing exactly that! And, further, this
uniting of apostates, heretics, cults, and eventually the pagan
religions of the world is a sign that we are rapidly approaching the end of the age.

BABYLON THE HARLOT

When you follow the rules of Bible interpretation it is not
very difficult to figure out who "Mystery, Babylon the Great,
the Mother of Harlots" is. The prophets were consistent in
their use of prophetic symbols. A woman used symbolically in
Scripture signifies religion. If it is a good woman it means a
good religion, such as "the bride," which is the Church. If it is
a bad woman, such as "the harlot," it means an evil religious
system that will deceive the souls of mankind.

"Babylon, the Mother of Harlots" is equally easy to understand, for Babylon was the source of all ancient idolatry.
What is obviously meant, then, is that in the Tribulation
period there will be a one-world idolatrous religion so powerful that it can exert pressure on the "beast," or political
leader of the day. Certainly we have a precedent for this in
the days when Roman Catholic popes were able to force
Roman emperors to do their will. So it will be during the

first half of the Tribulation period. Revelation 17 goes on to describe the ultimate destruction of this evil Babylonish religious system in the middle of the Tribulation period, but that is not germane to our study here.

This passage is of vital interest to us in that it prophecies a one-world religious system coming on the scene, amalgamating all the major religions of the world into one idolatrous system. It is my firm conviction that just such a system has been very active in the world for many years and is even now working inexorably toward the goal of "ecumenicity," or religious amalgamation.

Twenty-five years ago I preached a message on this subject during a prophetic series in our church. On the basis of what I believe to be the clear teaching of this prophecy, I made the prediction that "one of these days we will see apostate Protestant churches and the Roman Catholic Church make overtures toward getting together." At that time the theological chasm between them was so vast that it seemed impossible. Some of the folks who left the meeting said with a smile, "That young preacher has gotten carried away with the study of prophecy." But they don't smile any longer!

During these past twenty-five years we have seen a gradual and consistent change in both religious groups, producing a climate of cooperation between them that suggests total union within a few years. Consider some of the events which would have been considered impossible twenty-five years ago. After Vatican I and II, tremendous changes occurred in Catholicism. For instance, there has been a significant soft-pedaling of "Mariolatry," the doctrine which Protestants found most offensive. Pope John XXIII changed the Catholic attitude toward Protestants from that of "heretics" to "separated brethren," no small leap forward. Pope Paul VI liberalized the mass, and the Bible is now read and in many places taught in English from the pulpit.

For the first time we are hearing of Catholics who meet to study the Bible, as Protestants have done for years. In fact, I was recently amazed to hear a man from the Chicago area say after an evening service, "I like to hear you preach because you remind me of the priest I studied under before coming to California." He went on to explain that the similarities between us were that I spoke from the Bible and taught such things as "being born again" and "the Spirit-filled life." Would you have believed that twenty-five years ago? The 1989 Gallup Poll on religion indicates that as many as 13 million Roman Catholics in the United States alone profess to having "a born-again" experience with Jesus Christ.

What these changes in Catholicism indicate is that they are plagued with the same divisions that divides Protestantism. One group, the conservatives, believes the Bible to be the authoritative Word of God. The other group, the liberals, does not. That is why the liberal National or World Council of Churches takes the same stand on many moral, social, and theological issues as do the liberal Catholics. Liberation theology, a Marxist distortion of theology that originated in the Catholic church, is also popular in some liberal Protestant churches and is not much different than the theological teachings that have been offered in liberal seminaries and churches for years. After the Rapture has taken out of this world all true believers, it will be easy for the liberals that are left to close ranks and blend together into one worldwide federated church.

People have been amazed to find that all these changes in Catholicism reveal to the world the same divisions that have plagued Protestantism for three-quarters of a century, liberalism versus fundamentalism. But while all this was going on in the Church of Rome, the "separated brethren" were on a unity jag. Discarding doctrinal principle for organizational unity, large church groups began to merge under the guidance of leaders of the National Council of Churches of Christ in America. And more are being planned. The watchword seems to be, "We are all the children of God." Little attempt is made to define this God or to teach any particular way of pleasing him.

This spirit of togetherness has not been limited to Protestants. In the last few years I have seen things I never dreamed possible. An Arizona newspaper showed a Baptist minister and a Catholic priest jointly participating in a marriage ceremony. Equally as amazing was a report that a Catholic priest had attended the ordination of a Baptist minister. Interviewed afterward, he said that he had found it a "deeply moving experience." In addition, a common Bible for Catholics, Jews, and Protestants has been published and is doubtless going to contribute toward that common religious climate that will nurture the seeds of ecumenicity, particularly after the Church has been raptured. When our Lord calls all true believers from whatever church they are in to be with himself, the liberals in those churches will recognize they have too much in common with each other to remain apart. They will merge under the liberal leadership left in Rome. The other religions of the world will be brought in, and "Mystery, Babylon the Great, the Mother of Harlots and Abominations" (idolatry) of the earth will become awesomely powerful. *So* powerful, in fact, that she will be able to dominate the Antichrist's government during the first three-and-one-half years of the Tribulation period. That is why she is pictured in Revelation as a harlot riding the beast. The beast is the Antichrist's government, and her power is seen in that she is riding—meaning, in control. What is interesting to those who know the book of Revelation is that she will be the religious force that persecutes the 144,000 witnesses of Revelation 7 and murders their converts during that first three-and-one-half years of Tribulation

(Rev. 7:9-14). This religious system will be anti-Christian and will resort to the pagan religions of Babylon—the original source of all pagan religions. Even now the seeds for this all-purpose, anti-Christian religious plant have been sown and are growing rapidly. When fully developed, this false religious system will one day cover the entire world. You can be sure that this plant is growing into the biggest and strangest religious hybrid of all time.

Naturally, the World Council of Churches will get into the global act. At first it merely sent observers to Vatican I. Today it holds regular "dialogue" sessions. Now that the former head of the NCCCA has become leader of the World Council, he has a lofty platform for propagating his apostate doctrines and will doubtless work tirelessly for Catholic-Protestant unity.

PAGAN ECUMENICITY NEXT?

When the work of amalgamating Roman Catholicism and apostate Protestantism is complete, it won't be enough, for together they will number only one-quarter of the world's population. It should be remembered, however, that the one billion members of those two religious bodies have their roots in the countries of the old Roman government from which the ten-toed government of the Antichrist will come (to be studied in chapter 14). Even so, the differences between paganism and the ornate religious practices of some branches of Christendom are not as distinct as one might think. In India some years ago I visited several Hindu temples and Catholic churches. Frankly, I saw many similarities. The incense burning, sense of mystery, idolatrous images, superstition, and spirit of self-sacrifice to "please the gods" existed in both places. One missionary in South India said it was not uncommon for Indian Hindus to become Catholics and go right on worshiping in the Hindu religion.

Not only did it seem apparent to me that a simple procedure would merge Hinduism and Catholicism, but I found that Buddhism, an outgrowth of Hinduism, has many similar customs. It doesn't tax my credulity to believe that the day will soon come when Hinduism, Buddhism, Catholicism, apostate Protestantism, and who knows what else will combine. That would involve over three-fourths of the population of the world!

The reader should keep in mind that this amalgamation need not take place before the coming of Christ. It could very easily be accomplished right after the Antichrist signs a covenant with Israel to begin the Tribulation. The ecumenicized Church of Rome and Protestantism, with the government of the Antichrist to back it, could very quickly bring all the religions of the world into one gigantic tent, for they all have one thing in common — a religion of externals. Idolatry, which has always been the religious crutch of Satan to deceive the multitudes, undergirds them all. Someone once said, "The more religion a man has on the inside, the less he craves on the outside. But the less he has on the inside, the more he craves on the outside." Men who do not know the truth of Christ Jesus and lack his Spirit within crave elaborate external aids to worship. These idolatrous practices, therefore, will provide them a common denominator.

Humanly speaking, all that inhibits the ecumenical movement today are the evangelical, Bible-believing Christians. They take many forms and are found in many denominations, but thank God they exist. They are the group called "the Church" that Christ is coming for. Unfortunately, they are sadly divided, suspicious, and sometimes downright vicious toward each other. I use the term "Church" in the sense of believers in the fundamentals of the faith, i.e., the inspiration and infallibility of the Bible, the complete and unique deity of

Jesus Christ, and other cardinal doctrines. Naturally, this is an oversimplification, but for our purposes in this brief study it conveys the point that so-called Christendom is divided basically into two main groups: the apostates and the evangelicals.

Were it not for these Bible-believing Christians today, the leaders of the ecumenical movement would have proceeded much further than they have toward amalgamation of the denominations. One reason we know this is that Bible believers seem to be the only group hated by religious apostates. They speak tolerantly of criminals, Communists, Red China, amoralists, and social dropouts of every kind, but they shower all kinds of invective upon evangelicals.

It doesn't take too much imagination to see what will happen as soon as the true Church is taken out of this world by Christ at his coming. The inhibiting influence upon the ecumenical movement will be removed, and their cry, "We do better together," will unite the religious world.

TRY THE SPIRITS

The Church has never lacked enemies! From the very earliest days, apostates and a variety of heretics followed the apostles everywhere. Each of the latter books of the New Testament contains a warning against such characters who would seek to "creep in unawares" and lead people astray. For that reason the admonitions of the apostle John are particularly appropriate today and will continue to grow in significance as we get closer to the coming of Christ.

"Beloved, believe not every spirit, but try the spirits whether they are of God; because many false prophets are gone out into the world. Hereby know ye the Spirit of God: every spirit that confesseth that Jesus Christ is come in the flesh is of God; and every spirit that confesseth not that Jesus

Christ is come in the flesh is not of God; and this is that spirit of antichrist, whereof ye have heard that it should come, and even now already is it in the world. Ye are of God, little children, and have overcome them, because greater is he that is in you, than he that is in the world. They are of the world, therefore speak they of the world, and the world heareth them. We are of God. He that knoweth God heareth us. He that is not of God heareth not us. Hereby know we the spirit of truth, and the spirit of error" (1 John 4:1-6).

There is no reason for a Christian to be deceived by the tidal wave of anti-Christian teaching coming from religious leaders today if he knows his Bible, for he can "try the spirits." Because we are blessed with some excellent modern translations, like *The Living Bible,* the New King James Version, The New Revised Standard Version, and the *New American Standard Bible,* making the Scriptures easy to understand and apply to life, you owe it to yourself to study one. As we approach the end of this age and as the voices of apostasy and heresy become more prominent, make sure that you are not deceived. If you walk in the Spirit, feed daily on the Word of God, actively attend a Bible-believing church, and obey what the Holy Spirit directs you to do, you will have no problem. If you neglect the Word, you make yourself vulnerable to the deceiver who would, if possible, as Jesus warned, "deceive the very elect."

FOURTEEN
THE DISUNITED NATIONS— OR NEW WORLD ORDER

Another astounding evidence that we are in the last days just prior to the return of Christ is the shimmering glass tower beside the Hudson River in Manhattan, known as the United Nations Building. This gigantic exercise in futility has its roots deeply entrenched in World War I. Although an alert United States Senate rejected the first attempt of the "one-worlders" to enmesh America in the League of Nations after World War I, the internationalists never gave up. Finally, on October 24, 1945, their persistent campaign of education and intrigue was rewarded. The United States joined most of the other governments of the world in an organization that was supposed to bring "peace" to mankind.

No student of prophecy should have been surprised by that turn of events, for some of the most important prophetic passages in the Bible make it clear that two forms of one-world government will exist in the last days. The Satan-inspired government headed up by the Antichrist, the embodiment of evil, will last seven years, followed by the world government of righteousness, the utopia for which men have yearned. This final kingdom, described in Isaiah 65–66 and in Revelation 19–20, will be headed by Jesus Christ and will last a thousand years. It will give mankind the only rest from war the world has ever known.

Unlike Christ's Kingdom, which will be introduced dramatically and suddenly with his return to destroy the Antichrist, the satanic kingdom will come on the scene gradually. I believe that it is just around the corner.

DANIEL TELLS IT LIKE IT IS!

The prophet Daniel recorded two visions that are reaching their climax today; Nebuchadnezzar's image and vision of world governments in chapter 2, and Daniel's vision of world governments in chapter 7.

Nebuchadnezzar, monarch of the great Babylonian nation, dreamed of a beautiful image whose head was made of gold, arms of silver, belly of brass, and legs of iron with a mixture of iron and clay in the feet and toes. A stone came out of a mountain, struck the image, ground it to powder, and expanded to fill the whole earth.

That vision was interpreted to Daniel by God (2:36-45). Since Nebuchadnezzar was a king, God gave him a vision foretelling the four great empires that would follow Babylon. The kingdoms' identities were revealed to Daniel in a later vision (8:15-25). The head of gold represented Nebuchadnezzar's Babylonian kingdom, and the arms and shoulders the kingdoms of Media and Persia that would replace his. The belly of brass stood for the Greek kingdom of Alexander the Great. The legs of iron portended the Roman governmental system that became the model for so many nations. The iron toes mixed with clay could well speak of democracy, since man was made of crumbling clay. Certainly in these days we have several forms of representative government based on the Roman style of democracy.

The "stone cut without hands" that smashes the image in the vision can only mean the cataclysmic return of Christ to establish the righteous millennial kingdom which this world so desperately needs. Christ is referred to spiritually as "the Rock," suggesting strength and stability.

DANIEL'S VISION

Daniel not only interpreted King Nebuchadnezzar's vision, but he himself received one which he described in chapter 7. His vision was very similar in meaning to the image vision, although certain details differed. He saw four fierce beasts, each representing a world empire.

The Babylonian Empire. "The first was like a lion, and had eagle's wings; I beheld till the wings thereof were plucked, and it was lifted up from the earth, and made stand upon the feet as a man; and a man's heart was given to it" (Daniel 7:4).

The Medo-Persian Empire. "After this I beheld, and, lo, another, like a leopard, which had upon the back of it four wings of a fowl; the beast had also four heads, and dominion was given to it" (Daniel 7:6).

The Roman Empire. "After this I saw in the night visions, and, behold, a fourth beast, dreadful and terrible, and strong exceedingly, and it had great iron teeth; it devoured and broke in pieces, and stamped the residue with the feet of it; and it was diverse from all the beasts that were before it, and it had ten horns" (Daniel 7:7).

The Antichrist and the ten kings. "I considered the horns, and, behold, there came up among them another little horn, before whom there were three of the first horns plucked up by the roots; and, behold, in this horn were eyes like the eyes of man, and a mouth speaking great things" (Daniel 7:8).

The coming of Christ. "I saw in the night visions, and, behold, one like the Son of man came with the clouds of heaven, and came to the Ancient of days, and they brought him near before him. And there was given him dominion, and glory, and a kingdom, that all people, nations, and languages should serve him; his dominion is an everlasting dominion, which shall not pass away, and his kingdom that which shall not be destroyed" (Daniel 7:13-14).

A careful comparison of these two very important visions will reveal some fascinating details. First, the contrast between the visions is remarkable. Both describe successive world governments, but they reflect opposing viewpoints. Nebuchadnezzar gives the human view, which sets forth a beautiful image of man. Daniel the prophet relates God's picture of government as a series of rapacious beasts that forecast cruelty to mankind.

History reveals man's idealistic belief that government exists for his good, but such has seldom been the case. Instead, all governments have been cruel taskmasters, exploiting or enslaving mankind. Today's intellectuals who still insist that a massive world government would solve the world's problems don't realize that the more government we have, the less liberty we enjoy. In addition, they simply do not understand the depraved nature of man, for a world government necessitates a world dictator, and powerful monarchs have proven to be the greatest destroyers of life. As Lord Acton so cogently observed, "Power tends to corrupt; absolute power corrupts absolutely."

Another interesting comparison in the visions is their accurate portrayal of history. How could Daniel, living twenty-five hundred years ago, make such an accurate projection of history unless he was guided by God? He predicted more than five hundred years before Christ that prior to the establishment of his kingdom there would be four successive world kingdoms. History attests the accuracy of his prediction, for the Babylonians were conquered by the Medo-Persians, Alexander the Great replaced them, and the Romans supplanted the Greeks. I find it fascinating that there has never been a fifth world empire. Not that some have not tried. We have all read about Genghis Khan, Napoleon, Adolf Hitler, Joseph Stalin, and a host of other would-be world conquerors. They must not have known that God said there would only be four!

Another interesting thing about these visions is that both culminate in the Second Coming of Christ. He is truly God's hope for this earth.

Daniel's vision provides one detail omitted by Nebuchadnezzar which is of paramount importance to our study. In chapter 7, verse 8, he predicts that among the ten horns (corresponding with the ten toes of chapter 2) there is "a little horn" who plucks up three of the horns (or kings), and he has "eyes like the eyes of a man." With these words we are introduced to the one-world dictator who will come on the scene in the last days to rule the world for a short time.

The Antichrist is not a stranger to prophecy students, for he appears many times in the prophetic writings. Some of his other titles are: "a king of fierce countenance," "prince that shall come," "willful king," "son of perdition," "that wicked," and "a beast." From these we gather that he will be a wicked ruler who, in the tradition of those before him, will kill many people. In 7:21 Daniel indicates that he will particularly make war with the people of God.

THE UNIQUE FOURTH BEAST

Daniel's interpretation of the fourth beast, in verse 23, indicates that it is unique from all the others in that it would "devour the whole earth." That has never happened! None of the four kingdoms ever ruled the entire earth. They ruled the world known to western historians, but none went east of the Euphrates River. Since Roman government is still with us, we may conclude that she will yet rule this planet Earth. And I believe that she is on the verge of doing just that.

The Roman form of government is at the core of almost all governments today, from the so-called democracies to the dictatorships. Even the United Nations Charter has much in it that is of Rome. All that remains is for these independent governments to feel the need for a one-world government. And when world conditions permit or require, Rome will "devour the whole earth."

POSSIBLE COMING EVENTS

It is not difficult to understand how these events fit into our time. We have already seen that Russia and her northeastern confederation will go against Israel and be destroyed by God. A natural outcome would be the suggestion by world leaders: "Now that communism, the great deterrent to world peace, is destroyed, let us insure that there will be no more wars by turning all our armies over to the United Nations." World disarmament, a program already well planned by the U.N., would be implemented. We have the machinery for such a program right now. Once America has spent itself into bankruptcy defending the other countries of the world, as we did in the 1991 Middle East Gulf War, Russia and her "hordes" as Ezekiel calls them will be free to attack Israel according to Ezekiel 38 and 39.

The dream of world government on a voluntary basis will be short-lived, for it will break into ten kingdoms. At that point the Antichrist will subtly take power from each king and rule the world. How many of these events will take place before Christ comes for his Church, only God knows. But Christians should read the Bible and the daily newspaper with a spirit of anticipation, for the stage is being set for the most dramatic series of events in the history of the world.

THE FUTILITY OF THE UNITED NATIONS

That Christians are prone to look upon the idealism of the U.N. with suspicion and pessimism should not be surprising. Admittedly, the U.N. is an ingenious idea and has many lofty goals, but we predict its total failure on the authority of God's Word.

The most significant day in the history of the U.N. came in 1945, when, to appease the atheistic Communists, U.N. leaders decided to omit mention of God in the charter. That action signaled the death knell of the U.N. Jesus Christ said, "Without me, ye can do nothing." An organization that deliberately ignores the Creator is doomed to failure.

The U.N. is a classic example of the futility of man's efforts independent of God. It has attracted some of the keenest minds in the world, has had at its disposal the most advanced technology known to man, and has spent billions of dollars in the pursuit of world peace. Instead of world peace, however, history reveals that since the founding of the U.N. in 1945 we have experienced more wars on this planet than at any other comparable period of time. We are continually astonished that intelligent people do not comprehend that man will never solve his problems independent of God.

Someone sent me a beautiful color painting of the U.N.

headquarters building. Outside is a giant figure of Christ knocking for entrance. That picture dramatizes the futility of the U.N.

Governments tend to leave Christ out of their thinking because people leave him out of their lives. The same painting could be made showing Christ knocking at the door of every individual's heart. He is on the outside until invited in. He will not force his way in, but waits to be invited into their lives. If you haven't already done so, I encourage you to open the door of your heart and ask him to be your "way, truth, and life."

FIFTEEN
IS THIS THE
LAST GENERATION?

Since the day Jesus Christ ascended into heaven, no generation has had so much reason to believe it was the last one. A look at the chart on the next page will reveal that since the first great sign of our Lord's return there have been at least ten other signs. Each sign, or "birth pain" as suggested in Matthew 24:8, has become more intense, indicating that the moment of "travail" is at hand in this age.

The uniqueness of this prophetic book is the basing of these signs in the first great sign, World War I. Admittedly, some appeared prior to 1914, just as the conditions that produced the tragic war rumbled long before the opening Serbian shot was fired. But we must keep in mind that these signs are conditions that will crescendo in the Tribulation and they require time to develop. For example, the thinking pattern of mankind must be conditioned properly for a one-world government to form. The world was not ready for it in 1919, but the relentless conditioning process of the media and one-world globalism as taught in our school system has produced a generation that looks upon it as the only hope for mankind. This

ISRAEL

Ezek. 37

WORLD WAR I

Matt. 24:1-8

RISE OF RUSSIA

Ezek. 38-39

1914

FOUR PARTS
TO FIRST SIGN

1. WORLD WAR STARTED
   BY TWO NATIONS
2. FAMINES
3. PESTILENCE
4. MANY EARTHQUAKES
   AT ONCE

CAPITAL & LABOR
CONFLICT

James 5:1-6

INCREASE IN TRAVEL
AND KNOWLEDGE

Dan. 12:4

APOSTASY

2 Thess. 2:3

OCCULTISM

1 Tim. 4:1-2

ECUMENICAL CHURCH

Rev. 17

	TRIB.	MILLENNIUM

MORAL BREAKDOWN

2 Tim. 3:1-5

ONE WORLD GOVERNMENT

Dan. 2

SCOFFERS

2 Peter 3:1-12

sign could be fulfilled in a very brief time, and so it is with all the signs!

The stage is now set; the characters are in place; some minor "make-up" work might be done, but there is nothing major lacking before Christ comes for his Church. As we have noted, we *may* see Russian communism destroyed; we may see the one-world government; but we will not see the Antichrist sign the treacherous covenant with Israel — not if we are Christians.

To refer again to the illustration of a woman about to deliver her child, it would seem that the world is ready to rush to the delivery room for the seven-year ordeal of human travail.

As weighty as these accumulated signs are in suggesting the imminent coming of Christ, we have even clearer evidence from our Lord himself. We have only examined Matthew 24:1-8 so far; now it is time to finish the Lord's teaching on this subject. Before reading further, please examine the chart on pages 190 and 191, then read Matthew 24:1-36. Keep in mind that 24:9-31 reveals the sequence of future events, whereas verses 32-36 draw a significant conclusion based on this chronology.

It is time now to "learn a parable of the fig tree." Many prophecy students see this reference to "the fig tree beginning to bud" as meaning when you see the rise of Israel as a nation (as we did in 1948), you know that the time is "near." Their reasoning is that when a fig tree is used symbolically in Scripture, it usually refers to the nation of Israel. If that is a valid assumption, that Israel officially becoming a nation in 1948, as the culmination of the First World War sign of Matthew 24:1-8 (the first birth pain) — then it is "near" the time of the next major event of prophecy — which is the return of Christ. It is interesting that after nineteen hundred years of wandering around the world homeless that Israel started back into the land as a result of World War I in 1914. She was not a nation, of course, until thirty-four years later when she was officially recognized by the United Nations. It was as if the tree was planted in 1914–1918 when the first "birth pain" was felt, but did not grow into a full-blown tree that could bud until 1948 when Israel was granted statehood — thus fulfilling Ezekiel 37.

If indeed this is what our Lord had in mind when designating "the fig tree" in Matthew 24:32, then we can assume that we are "in the season" of our Lord's coming. For He said: "So likewise ye, when ye shall see all these things, know that it is near. . . ." In other words, when all the signs mentioned appear — World War I, famines, pestilence, earthquakes, and Israel becoming a nation — you know that Jesus' return is near, even at the doors.

THESE THINGS

There are two sets of "these things" in verses 33 and 34. If you fail to distinguish between them, you will not understand what our Lord said. On the chart I have marked them these things "#1" and these things "#2." They are definitely not the same. The first "these things" in verse 33 refers back to the tumultuous events begun by verses 7 and 8. The second "these things" refers to the prophetic future, including the Tribulation and the glorious appearing of Christ.

Our Lord's meaning in verses 32 and 33, then, is that just as a tree's buds indicate summer is coming, so "these things #1" would mean the Lord's coming is near, "even at the doors." We can thus know the season of his return.

Great care should be taken not to set dates in this connection. Jesus said, "But of that day and hour knoweth no man, no, not the angels of heaven, but the Father only" (verse 36). The study of prophecy has probably suffered more from date

MATTHEW 24:1-36

The Sign of the End of the Age
World War I (1914-1918)

"Wars and Rumors of Wars"
"False Christs"

CHURCH AGE

| 24:1-3 | 4-6 | 7 |

#1
1. WORLD WAR
2. PESTILENCE
3. FAMINE
4. EARTHQUAKES (v. 7)
5. ISRAEL, THE FIG TREE,
   BEGINS TO BUD
   (v. 32)

The Glorious Appearing of Christ
(55vv. 27-31)

7 YRS. TRIBULATION	MILLENNIUM KINGDOM OF CHRIST

8   9-26

"THIS GENERATION
(THAT SEES #1)
SHALL NOT PASS 'TIL
ALL THESE THINGS
BE FULFILLED" (#2)

#2
1. TRIBULATION
2. ARMAGEDDON
3. CHRIST COMING
(v. 34)

setters than anything else. On the other hand, this passage clearly indicates we can know the season. It is my firm belief that we are not only in the season, but in the latter portion of it. We must not, however, make our interpretation any more specific than the Lord makes his prophecy. As we shall see, he indicated that the season could last as long as a generation.

THE KEY GENERATION

Now we are ready to examine the key to this whole passage as it relates to the time of Jesus' coming, in answer to the disciples' question: "When shall these things be?" The key is found in verse 34. Jesus said, "This generation shall not pass, till all these things [#2] be fulfilled." The crucial issue, then, concerns the meaning of "this generation," for whatever generation he had in mind would not pass until the Second Coming occurs. There seem to be only three generations from which to choose.

1. *The disciples' generation*—but nothing like that happened historically during their lifetime, and their generation has passed and obviously the Lord has not come, so it doesn't seem possible he had their generation in mind.

2. *The generation that saw the First World War* was thought by many fine Bible teachers forty years ago to be a possibility. That scenario becomes increasingly unlikely today in that most of that generation has already passed away—although there are still some ninety-seven-plus-year-old people alive and well. That possibility should not be ruled out completely for another five years or so.

3. *The generation that saw Israel officially become a nation in 1948.* That is, the generation that was old enough to "see" the pictures via television or newsreel of the United Nations officially recognize Israel as a nation. Assuming that meant children ten years of age or older in 1948, it probably means the

generation born around 1938 — give or take five or ten years.

In Greek the demonstrative pronoun *haute* (this) always refers to the person or thing mentioned before it. The thing mentioned just before "generation" involves those who see the sign of Israel becoming a nation.

Carefully putting all this together, we now recognize this strategic generation. It is the generation that "sees" the events of 1948. We must be careful here not to become dogmatic, but it would seem that these people are witnesses to the events, not necessarily participants in them. That would suggest they were at least old enough to understand the events of 1948.

I believe it is that generation which our Lord said "will not pass away till all those things [#2] be fulfilled."

HOW LONG IS A GENERATION?

We may logically inquire next, "How long is a generation?" Psalm 90:10 provides insight into this subject. "The days of our years are three-score years and ten; and if, by reason of strength, they be four-score years, yet is their strength labor and sorrow. . . ." This does not mean that the final generation is limited to seventy or eighty years; the psalmist is acquainting us with the general length of a generation.

We should weigh the Lord's words very carefully here. He said, "This generation shall not pass until all these things be fulfilled." How many people make up a generation? No particular number; just one person who comprehended the significant events of 1948 could represent the "generation." Jesus was aware that the last generation before his coming would be marked by longevity. We are acquainted with ninety-year-old people, so "this generation" is not limited to eighty years. However, neither should we expect the entire generation to pass away before Jesus returns!

HOW MUCH LONGER DO WE HAVE?

All of us know gray-haired members of the generation that witnessed the events of 1948. If indeed this is the generation our Lord had in view, and that does seem probable, we do not have much more time on earth. I refuse to set any date limits, for the Lord didn't, but he did specify a generation's experiences and said that he would return during that period. We are in the twilight of that generation — that I firmly believe. How much longer God will spare this world, only he knows. But if ever there was a generation that should live every moment as though Christ is about to come, it is this one.

If you think the above teachings indicate that time is short, you are right. But if you are a Christian, keep in mind that Christ is coming to take his people seven years *before* the end of the age. So, whatever conclusion you come to about "the end of the age," the Christians' departure comes seven years earlier.

Unbelievers will have up to seven additional years after Christians leave, but it will be the worst years of their lives. It is risky, if not fatal, to wait until Christ has taken his Church out of the world before becoming a Christian. Paul warns in 2 Thessalonians 2:9-12 that people who know the truth about Christ and reject him will be deceived into believing the false messiah of the end time.

So we are forced to make a decision about Christ while we have the opportunity. "Now is the accepted time; today is the day of salvation." I urge you to invite him into your life if you have never done so.

SIXTEEN
ANTICIPATING THE END

There is no question that we are living in the last days. The Bible passages we have examined make that very clear. It is fascinating to us who have preached this for years to hear the growing chorus of voices that declare the same thing.

Twenty years ago, the president of the World Bank called attention to the population explosion that was alarming world economists. Pointing out that sixteen hundred years were required to double the first-century population from 125 million to 250 million, he stated, "Today, the more than three billions on earth will double in thirty-five years. To project the totals beyond the year 2000 becomes so demanding on the imagination as to make the statistics almost incomprehensible."[1]

Economists make it clear that technology is not keeping pace with population, and we are rapidly approaching the time when we will not be able to feed the people on earth. Already some parts of the world have malnourished masses who are reproducing more hungry millions, with no solution in sight.

Pollution experts warn that if something drastic is not done soon, we will smother earth life. Pollution has plagued large cities for years, but in recent times it has reached dangerous proportions. Can you imagine the pollution if the present population doubles in thirty-five years?

China now has nuclear weapons and is working for a delivery system. No thinking person wishes to predict the frightening possibilities that await this world when that happens. One political scientist on a TV interview, when asked his view of life in the twenty-first century, said, "Pardon my pessimism, but when I think of China's nuclear development in the light of their past, I see no future for the known world beyond the year 2000."

Since that statement, five other nations have obtained nuclear weapons, bringing the known nations with nuclear capabilities to at least eight. We all know that the ruthless Saddam Hussein was within three years of possessing nuclear weapons. There is no way to indefinitely keep terrorists or dictators without moral values from eventually threatening the entire world with nuclear blackmail. Only an enforceable one-world government with an autocratic dictator will keep this nuclear world from destroying this world someday — and one is coming and his name is Antichrist! But he will not come until *after* Christ has returned for his Church.

We could cite other trends in the field of travel, knowledge, technology, dope addiction, and family breakdown — mankind is on a runaway course that portends the end of this age. Just such an end has been prophesied by God.

GET READY

Most people don't heed warnings. The people of Noah's day disregarded his warnings for 120 years — then they were swept away in the Flood. Jesus warned our generation, "Therefore, be ye also ready; for in such an hour as ye think not the Son of man cometh" (Matthew 24:44). That challenge is for our generation!

The fact that we are the generation that will be on earth when our Lord comes certainly should not depress us. In fact, the depressing conditions presently ensnaring our society should not make us despondent. Instead, we should anticipate the Lord's coming every day.

Shortly after the death of Dr. M. R. DeHaan, the much-loved radio Bible teacher and capable prophecy student, I visited his study. Behind his desk was a framed wall sign that read, "Perhaps Today!" That mental attitude should characterize every believer.

If you knew when the world was going to be destroyed, would you warn everyone you could to get ready? Of course you would. Well, if you are a Christian, after reading this book you ought to know that the end is near!

The time for waiting to witness to our loved ones and friends is past; they need a warning today. If we compare our days to Noah's, I would say the storm clouds are gathering. Soon the door to survival, Jesus the Christ, is going to be closed, and God will thunder judgment upon this generation. If listeners heed your warning, they will be eternally grateful; if they reject it, they will experience ultimate despair. But it is high time we Christians recognize that we are in the warning business.

Several Christian leaders have recently shared an observation that confirms my own — an increasing number of people, many of whom once rejected the gospel of Christ, are now open to God's message. Actually, what else is there for people to do? An engineer with whom I shared Christ recently said, "I resisted everything you said because it conflicted with all I have been taught, but I received Christ because it suddenly dawned on me that there is no alternative. Now for the first time I have a peace I never dreamed possible."

Everywhere we go there are empty-hearted college and

high school kids, parents, couples, and grandparents who are seeking peace in drugs, sex, amusement, alcohol, and a host of other things. What they need, of course, is Christ, and it is our job to warn them to get ready.

Six weeks after my wife and I were married, we were driving across the country. As we approached the Mississippi River, an old man waved us down with a red flag. I must confess, I was a little irritated at the old gent because he was throwing my time schedule off. But my irritation vanished when I heard him exclaim, "The bridge is out!" That man saved our lives because he was faithful in warning us that the highway came to an abrupt end.

Mankind is racing down the highway of life oblivious to its sudden end; the Christians' job is to wave the warning flag and tell them: "Be ye also ready; for in such an hour as ye think not the Son of man cometh."

1. Robert S. McNamara, "World Dilemma," *Commander's Digest,* May 31, 1969.

Other Prophecy books by Dr. LaHaye

Life in the Afterlife

Revelation Illustrated and Made Plain

How to Study Bible Prophecy for Yourself

The Coming Peace in the Middle East

A catalogue of these and other books and tapes is available by writing:

Family Life Ministries
P. O. Box 2700
Washington, DC 20013

The Washington Prophecy Report by Dr. Tim LaHaye is a timely interpretation of currents events evaluated in the light of Bible prophecy. From his office on Capitol Hill in Washington, D.C., Dr. LaHaye is able to keep on top of fast-breaking international news stories and events that are of interest to the student of Bible prophecy. You will find the *The Washington Prophecy Report* in either print or cassette message form to be an ideal way to keep on the cutting edge of prophetically significant events — as *the day* approaches.

In addition, Dr. LaHaye produces a printed version of the *Capital Report* — a monthly selection of some of his daily commentaries for radio and TV, giving a Christian conservative comment on events of interest to Christians, the church, and the family. A free sample is available upon request.